The Critical Idiom
General Editor: JOHN D. JUMP

14 *Allegory*

Allegory / *John MacQueen*

Methuen & Co Ltd

For HECTOR

First published 1970
by Methuen & Co Ltd
11 New Fetter Lane London EC4
© 1970 John MacQueen
Printed in Great Britain
by Cox & Wyman Ltd, Fakenham, Norfolk

SBN   416   08040   5 Hardback
SBN   416   08050   2 Paperback

Distributed in the U.S.A.
by Barnes & Noble Inc.

Contents

General Editor's Preface

This volume is one of a series of short studies, each dealing with a single key item, or a group of two or three key items, in our critical vocabulary. The purpose of the series differs from that served by the standard glossaries of literary terms. Many terms are adequately defined for the needs of students by the brief entries in these glossaries, and such terms will not be the subjects of studies in the present series. But there are other terms which cannot be made familiar by means of compact definitions. Students need to grow accustomed to them through simple and straightforward but reasonably full discussions of them. The purpose of this series is to provide such discussions.

Some of the terms in question refer to literary movements (e.g., 'Romanticism', 'Aestheticism', etc.), others to literary kinds (e.g., 'Comedy', 'Epic', etc.), and still others to stylistic features (e.g., 'Irony', 'The Conceit', etc.). Because of this diversity of subject-matter, no attempt has been made to impose a uniform pattern upon the studies. But all authors have tried to provide as full illustrative quotation as possible, to make reference whenever appropriate to more than one literature, and to compose their studies in such a way as to guide readers towards the short bibliographies in which they have made suggestions for further reading.

John D. Jump

University of Manchester

I

Greek and Roman Allegory

The origins of allegory are philosophic and theological rather than literary. Most of all perhaps they are religious. From the beginning, however, allegory has been closely associated with narrative. All western and many eastern religions have found their most perfect expression in myth – a narrative, that is to say, or series of narratives which serves to explain those universal facts which most intimately affect the believer, facts such as times, seasons, crops, tribes, cities, nations, birth, marriage, death, moral laws, the sense of inadequacy and failure and the sense of potential, both of which characterize the greater part of mankind.

Those myths are transmitted, orally at first or in ritual, eventually sometimes by way of the written word. Often they are mysteries, the interpretation of which is revealed only to a priesthood, or to a larger body of initiates whose understanding is to be obtained by way of elaborate, sometimes dangerous or painful, ceremonial. Sometimes too there are degrees of initiation, with full enlightenment reserved for those who reach the highest level. Yet the myth could not have come into being without some interpretation, and it is reasonable to assume that from prehistoric times onwards myth and interpretation went hand in hand. Provided that a sequence of historical events was felt to have a special relevance to a particular society or group of people within a society, a myth might perfectly well have a basis in historical fact. The more extensive the group, the greater the power of the myth.

Examples are not difficult to find. If for instance we restrict ourselves to the classical world of Greece and Rome, the myth of Ceres and Proserpine (in Greek, Demeter and Persephone), which in the seventeenth century still retained its power over the imagination of Shakespeare (*Winter's Tale* IV iv, 116–27) and Milton:

> Not that fair field
> Of *Enna*, where *Proserpin* gath'ring flow'rs
> Herself a fairer Flow'r by gloomy *Dis*
> Was gather'd, which cost *Ceres* all that pain
> To seek her through the world
>
> > (*Paradise Lost* IV, 268–72)

began as an allegorical explanation of the process of sowing and harvesting corn. By an almost inevitable extension, it became an allegory of human immortality, or perhaps rather rebirth, after death. In a sense, both Ceres and her daughter Proserpine *are* the corn. This is more obviously true of Proserpine, but in Latin poetry, for instance, the word Ceres is sometimes used simply to mean 'corn', as by Virgil in *Aeneid* I, 177–9, when he describes the meal prepared by Aeneas's companions after the storm which had so nearly shipwrecked them:

> *tum Cererem corruptam undis Cerialiaque arma*
> *expediunt fessi rerum, frugesque receptas*
> *et torrere parant flammis et frangere saxo.*

(Then, weary of life, they fetch out Ceres, spoiled by the waves, and the arms of Ceres [i.e. the implements for grinding and baking] and prepare to bake the recovered grain and to crush it with a grindstone.)

In Greek likewise the word Demeter is used to mean bread. At this level, Dis or Pluto, the god of the underworld who rapes Proserpine, is the earth in which the seed is buried and germinates. At a different level, however, Dis is death, and Proserpine is the human soul, subject to death, but redeemed by the toils of the mother goddess, Ceres. For a Greek, initiation into the mystery of Demeter at Eleusis near Athens probably involved the revelation of just this level of meaning.

Here then we already have two levels of allegorical interpretation, one which the late Greek philosopher, Sallustius, whose work is discussed below, would probably have called 'material' and one which he would have called 'psychic'. As I have said, both levels remained familiar and were still used by English poets at a comparatively recent date. Pope makes use of the material level (and incidentally imitates Virgilian usage), when he writes:

> Another age shall see the golden ear
> Imbrown the slope and nod on the parterre,
> Deep harvests bury all his pride has plann'd,
> And laughing Ceres reassume the land.
> (*Moral Epistles* IV, 'The Use of Riches', 173–6)

Milton in the passage just quoted uses the psychic level. His reference occurs in the description of Paradise as first seen by Satan when he is perched in the form of a cormorant on the Tree of Life. In terms of the poem, the rape of Proserpine corresponds to the fall of Adam and Eve, Dis is equivalent to Satan, and Ceres to Christ the Redeemer. The general subject of the poem is Man's first disobedience, which

> Brought Death into the World, and all our woe
> With loss of *Eden*, till one greater Man
> Restore us, and regain the blissful Seat.
> (*Paradise Lost* I, 3–5)

Milton makes the comparison primarily because Enna was a place of legendary beauty like that of Paradise, but he knew the allegorical interpretation, an understanding of which enhances the reader's imaginative and intellectual experience.

A later classical myth which never, in all probability, possessed an interpretation at the material level, is that of the search through the underworld by the musician Orpheus for his dead wife Eurydice. The search in the earliest versions was probably successful, but in later versions Orpheus failed when, at the very instant of success, he glanced backwards. The myth was central to the mystic and philosophic Orphic cult in classical Greece. The allegory is psychic. Orpheus and his music represent the higher intellectual and redemptive powers of the human soul, Eurydice the lower, more appetitive powers which are particularly subject to evil and death. The sufferings of Orpheus in the upper and underworlds represent the sacrifices necessary if the soul is to redeem the lower self which it loves, and without which it cannot find salvation. The origin of the story may, as E. R. Dodds has suggested, lie in shamanistic beliefs and practices, but by classical Greek times, the main emphasis certainly fell on redemption, on salvation.

This emphasis in turn made it easy for theologians at a later date to treat the myth as an allegory of Christian redemption. An elaborate specimen of this Christian interpretation in one of its many forms is to be found in the *Orpheus and Eurydice* of the Scottish poet, Robert Henryson (c. 1420–90). Two centuries later, Milton made incidental use of it in his *Paradise Lost*. The passage occurs in the address to light at the beginning of Book III. Milton, as narrator of the infernal scenes which form a necessary prelude to the fall and salvation of man, compares himself, with some advantage, to Orpheus:

> Escap't the *Stygian* Pool, though long detain'd
> In that obscure sojourn, while in my flight
> Through utter and through middle darkness borne
> With other notes than to th' *Orphean* Lyre
> I sung of *Chaos* and *Eternal Night*,
> Taught by the heav'nly Muse to venture down
> The dark descent, and up to reascend,
> Though hard and rare.
>
> (III, 14–21)

(In classical tradition, it should be noted, Orpheus was the son of the Muse, Calliope.)

Under Orphic influence, the allegorical journey through the underworld became an essential part of classical epic poetry. The

development is seen at its most powerful in Virgil's *Aeneid*. Here
Aeneas arrives in Italy, stained with the guilt of his passionate
involvement with Dido at Carthage, stained too, in a more ritual
way, by the deaths of his comrades Palinurus and Misenus. To
obtain purification, and to enable him to carry out the divine purpose of founding Rome, it is necessary that he should make the
descent to Hades and return purified to his task in this world. The
descent to Hades is easy, but the re-ascent almost impossible:

> *facilis descensus Averno:*
> *noctes atque dies patet atri ianua Ditis;*
> *sed revocare gradum superasque evadere ad auras,*
> *hoc opus, hic labor est.*

(VI, 126–9)

The descent to Avernus is easy: night and day the door of black Dis
stands open; but to retrace one's step and escape to the upper air – this
is the work, this the difficulty.

The descent of Aeneas is an allegory of the dark night of the soul
as it is tempered to become the instrument of divine purpose.
Milton clearly had the Virgilian as well as the Orphic allegory in
mind when he wrote the address to light.

Very noticeably, Robert Henryson, in the poem to which I have
already referred, sends Orpheus on a journey, not through the
underworld only, but also through the upper world of the planetary spheres. His major emphasis is on the music, the harmony of
the spheres:

> Thair leirit he tonis proportionat . . .
> This mirry musik and mellefluat,
> Compleit and full of nummeris od and evin,
> Is causit be the moving of the hevin.

(219, 230–2)

In the cosmos, the music of the spheres corresponds to the harmony
of intellect in the little world of man, a harmony allegorically

represented by Orpheus's harp and its music. The journey through the spheres prepares him for the attempt to redeem the disharmonies of the underworld. Nor is Henryson's treatment unique. By his time the journey through the spheres had become as common a feature of post-classical epic and narrative poetry as the underworld journey had been of the classical. One may instance the *Anticlaudianus* of the twelfth century Latin poet, Alan of Lille, or at a later date the Mutability Cantos of Spenser's *Faerie Queene*. (These were published in 1609, ten years after Spenser's death.) Often the two journeys, underworld and upperworld, are combined, as in the *Divina Commedia* of Dante Alighieri (1265–1321), with its three parts, *Inferno* (underworld), *Purgatorio* (transition) and *Paradiso* (upperworld). As a musician, Milton was particularly sensitive to such allegory, as may equally be seen in his early poem, 'At a Solemn Music', and in the fine verbal detail of the much later *Paradise Lost*. It is not, for instance, mere delight in his own verbal skill which makes him attempt in these verses to catch the contrasted sounds of the gates of Hell and of Heaven:

> On a sudden op'n fly
> With impetuous recoil and jarring sound
> Th' infernal doors, and on thir hinges grate
> Harsh Thunder, that the lowest bottom shook
> Of *Erebus*.
>
> (II, 879–83)

> Heav'n op'n'd wide
> Her ever-during Gates, Harmonious sound
> On golden Hinges moving, to let forth
> The King of Glory in his powerful Word
> And Spirit coming to create new Worlds.
>
> (VII, 205–9)

The difference is itself an allegory of the intellectual gulf which separates the inhabitants of Hell from those of Heaven. Satan passes the infernal gates on a mission of destruction; the heavenly gates open to allow the Son to create a new universe. The music of the heavenly gates is directly related to the music of the spheres.

Henryson indicates the classical source of the allegory when in line 225 of his poem he refers to Plato and the doctrine that the harmony of the spheres is the *Anima Mundi*, Soul of the World, which Plato sets out in his *Timaeus*. Plato (427–348 B.C.) is in fact the effective founder of many aspects of the allegorical tradition. For a philosopher he was uncharacteristically aware of the limitations of human reason and knowledge. As a consequence, many of his dialogues include 'myths', allegorical narratives or developed metaphors, which serve to image truths beyond the reach of the discursive intellect. Many deal with the human soul. The *Phaedrus* provides an uncomplicated instance, when the soul is compared to a charioteer driving two steeds, one representing the spiritual, the other the sensual element in man, which the charioteer (reason) has to restrain. The *Symposium* contains a whole series of allegories, in different styles, on the subject of love.

In the *Republic*, the myth of the cave demonstrates the impossibility for the soul of reaching absolute knowledge so long as it is imprisoned by the fetters of sensual and corporeal life:

> Every feature in this parable, my dear Glaucon, is meant to fit our earlier analysis. The prison dwelling (the cave) corresponds to the region revealed to us through the sense of sight, and the firelight within it to the power of the Sun. The ascent to see the things in the upper world you may take as standing for the upward journey of the soul into the region of the intelligible.
>
> (VII 517. Cornford's translation, p. 226)

Plato talks here of an ascent to see the things in the upper world; he was also a mathematician and a Pythagorean, for whom it was natural to believe in the doctrine of the link between the harmony of the spheres and the philosophic harmony of the universe. The full identification of the two is to be found in another myth from the *Republic*, the famous vision of Er with which the dialogue

closes. Plato here combines the Orphic journey through the underworld with a vision of the harmony of the spheres represented by
the whorl on the spindle of Necessity:

> The whorl was of this fashion. In shape it was like an ordinary whorl;
> but from Er's account we must imagine it as a large whorl with the
> inside completely scooped out, and within it a second smaller whorl,
> and a third and a fourth and four more, fitting into one another like
> a nest of bowls . . . The Spindle turned on the knees of Necessity.
> Upon each of its circles stood a Siren, who was carried round with its
> movement, uttering a single sound on one note, so that all the eight
> made up the concords of a single scale. Round about, at equal dis-
> tances, were seated, each on a throne, the three daughters of Necessity,
> the Fates, robed in white with garlands on their heads, Lachesis,
> Clotho and Atropos, chanting to the Sirens' music, Lachesis of things
> past, Clotho of the present, and Atropos of things to come.
>
> (X 616-7. Cornford's translation, pp. 345-6)

The eightfold whorl is made up of the eight harmonious spheres of
the fixed stars, Saturn, Jupiter, Mars, Mercury, Venus, the Sun and
the Moon. The entire material universe, in other words, is merely
the whorl on the spindle, which rotates in time to the song of the
Fates, and spins the thread of Necessity. For almost every part of
existence, human beings, in Plato's opinion, are subjected completely to the power of Necessity and the Fates, but before the
beginning of an incarnation, each has the free opportunity of
choosing a lot, which settles the terms of his destiny, at least for
one incarnation. Plato may have taken his concept of the spheres
as themselves an allegory of Fate and Necessity from astrological
and deterministic sources, but he is careful to retain a place for
human free-will.

Er does not exactly make a journey through the upper world; he
is taken to a place from which he is able to see its structure. In the
dream narrative which forms a surviving part of the lost sixth book
of the *De Republica* of the Roman orator and statesman, Cicero

(106–43 B.C.), and which is generally known as the *Somnium Scipionis* (Dream of Scipio), Scipio Aemilianus, the adoptive grandson of the great Scipio Africanus, is taken by his grandfather to 'a certain place high up, glorious and bright, set thick with stars' (the Milky Way, that is to say), from which he sees the structure of the universe below, and where he learns the lesson of universal order and harmony. It was probably by way of the *Somnium Scipionis*, which itself derives from Plato's vision of Er, that medieval western Europe derived its idea of the allegorical journey through the heavens. Macrobius Theodosius, a Roman writer who flourished about A.D. 400, wrote a Neoplatonic commentary on the *Somnium Scipionis* which was well known to the Middle Ages, and which added precision to the discussion of the soul and its destiny in the light of doctrines propounded by the late Greek philosophers Plotinus (A.D. 205–69/70), and Porphyry (A.D. 232/3–305).

Some Platonic myths, it should be added, reveal a kinship with the fables attributed to the sixth century B.C. Greek, Aesop. Plato's teacher, Socrates, is said to have put some of those fables into verse during his imprisonment, and Plato, at the beginning of the *Phaedo* makes him tell a brief fable in the style of Aesop to illustrate the paradoxical relationship between pleasure and pain. Aesop's fables were generally animal stories with a moralizing application to human life (for instance, 'The Fox who lost his Tail'); some however dealt directly with day to day experience ('The Shepherd who reared Wolfcubs' or 'The Widow of Ephesus'), or indeed with inanimate nature ('The Fir-tree and the Thornbush', 'The North Wind and the Sun').

The most elaborate literary development of classical allegory is to be found in a late Latin novel, the *Golden Ass* or *Metamorphoses* of Lucius Apuleius, a north African rhetorician, philosopher and magician who lived in the second century A.D. As a consequence of his unusual beliefs and interests, the moral terms within which Apuleius made his allegory function are relatively difficult for present day readers. William Adlington, the sixteenth century English translator of Apuleius, expresses them thus:

> The argument of the book is, how Lucius Apuleius, the author himself, travelled into Thessaly (being a region in Greece where all the women for the most be such wonderful witches, that they can transform men into the figure of brute beasts) where after he had continued a few days, by the mighty force of a violent confection he was changed into a miserable ass, and nothing might reduce him to his wonted shape but the eating of a rose, which, after the endurance of infinite sorrow, at length he obtained by prayer. Verily under the wrap of this transformation is taxed the life of mortal men, when as we suffer our minds so to be drowned in the sensual lusts of the flesh and the beastly pleasures thereof (which aptly may be called the violent confection of witches) that we lose wholly the use of reason and virtue, which properly should be in a man, and play the parts of brute and savage beasts . . . But as Lucius Apuleius was changed into his human shape by a rose, the companions of Ulysses by great intercession, and Nebuchadnezzar by the continual prayers of Daniel, whereby they knew themselves and lived after a good and virtuous life: so can we never be restored to the right figure of ourselves, except we taste and eat the sweet rose of reason and virtue, which the rather by mediation of prayer we may assuredly attain.
>
> (*Apuleius*, ed. Gaselee, pp. xvi–xvii)

A few lines later Adlington expresses the same interpretation more briefly:

> This book of Lucius is a figure of man's life, and toucheth the nature and manners of mortal men, egging them forward from their asinal form to their human and perfect shape, beside the pleasant and delectable jests therein contained.

The briefer, more hedonistic, allegory of Cupid and Psyche, which occupies the greater part of Books IV, V and VI of Apuleius's novel, will serve to introduce another development of classical allegory. The divine names, Cupid and Psyche, are transparent personifications – *cupido* is a Latin abstract noun meaning 'desire, love';

Psyche is Greek ψυχή, and means 'soul'. The name Venus of the mother of Cupid is another abstract, meaning 'charm, beauty, sexual love', and *Voluptas*, the name of the child born to Cupid and Psyche, means 'pleasure'. The story gains meaning from the fact that it is concerned with personified abstractions treated as divinities. Psyche, soul, engages in a conflict with Venus, sensual passion, for union with Cupid, love. To win the conflict, it is necessary for her to suffer complete humiliation and to go as far as the waters of the Styx, the boundaries of death. But she is helped by the natural powers, associated with Ceres and Juno, and by the divine will, represented by Jupiter's eagle, and she finally triumphs. It is perhaps characteristic of the magical orientation of Apuleius's philosophy that the child born to the union of Psyche with Cupid should be, not Wisdom or Holiness, but Pleasure.

Apuleius is a relatively late writer, but his abstract divinities belong to a tradition fully established by the time of Hesiod, who probably lived in the eighth century B.C. The legend of Prometheus, for instance, which figures prominently in both the *Works and Days* and the *Theogony* is almost entirely peopled by abstractions. The name Prometheus means 'forethought'. He is the son of Themis (Justice) and brother of Epimetheus (Afterthought), whose wife is Pandora, an ambiguous name meaning both the Giver of All and the All-endowed. Prometheus, as Forethought, is a culture-hero, the master-craftsman who made the first men and gifted them with fire. He is also the trickster, capable of outwitting Zeus, the king of the gods, who in revenge created Pandora, the first woman. Her gifts are the evils which afflict humanity, and the single blessing, Hope. Deucalion, the son of Prometheus, married Pyrrha, the daughter of Epimetheus, and it was by the forethought of Prometheus that the pair were enabled to survive the flood with which Zeus had intended to destroy the human race. Most of the characters of the legend, all this is to say, are personifications of

B

aspects either of the human personality, or of the divine dispensation, which is seen as grudging, and indeed downright hostile to
human beings. Aeschylus (515–456 B.C.) maintained the emphasis
on abstraction when in his play, *Prometheus Bound*, he introduced
Kratos and Bia (Strength and Force), who appear in *Theogony* 385
as the inseparable companions of Zeus, to bring Prometheus to be
nailed to a rock in the Caucasus.

Hesiod's myths, on the whole, allegorize the attitudes of a peas-
ant rather than an aristocratic society towards the governing forces
of the universe. It may be significant of the same background that
Prometheus figures in the corpus of Aesopic fable.

From the time of Alexander the Great (356–323 B.C.), the importance of abstract divinities, and so of allegory, in Greek religious
beliefs steadily increased. Especially notable are the Stoic Φύσις,
translated by the Romans as *Natura*, Nature (or, in the useful
medieval terminology, Kind), and Τύχη, Latin *Fortuna* or *Sors*,
Fortune. As Ernst Curtius and others have shown, the whole later
development of imaginative literature is affected by those figures.
Combined with this was a tendency to etymologize the names of
originally non-abstract divinities into abstractions. The name of
the Greek Kronos (Κρόνος), equated by the Romans with Saturn,
was derived from χρόνος (chronos), time, and so he became Father
Time. Isidore of Seville (c.570–636) etymologized the name Saturn
in this way; *Hunc Latini a satu appellatum ferunt, quasi ad ipsum
satio omnium pertineat rerum, vel a temporis longitudine, quod
saturetur annis*, 'The Latins say that his name is derived from the
word *satus*, "sowing", as if the planting of all creation properly
appertains to him, or that it is derived from his extreme old age,
because he is saturated with years' (*Etymologiae*, VIII, xi, 30). It
should perhaps be added that none of those derivations is likely to
be accurate.

Already at a date much earlier than Isidore's, the treatment of the
gods as abstractions and the etymologizing of their names had

become two principal weapons of defence for poetry in her quarrel with philosophy – a quarrel which Plato in the *Republic* began by demonstrating the moral need to control children's reading:

> Stories like those of Hera being bound by her son, or of Hephaestus flung from heaven by his father for taking his mother's part when she was beaten, and all those battles of the gods in Homer, must not be admitted into our state, whether they be allegorical or not. A child cannot distinguish the allegorical sense from the literal, and the ideas he takes in at that age are likely to become indelibly fixed.
>
> (II 378. Cornford's translation, pp. 68–9)

He did not, it is obvious, have much confidence in allegorical interpretations (with which, equally obviously, he was familiar), and later in the *Republic* he proposed a total expulsion of poets and their works from an ideal commonwealth. The best known rejoinder to Plato, that of Aristotle in the *Poetics*, avoided allegorical interpretation as a defence by concentrating on the emotional effect of poetry in general and tragedy in particular, and so producing the famous doctrine of catharsis. Throughout the ancient world however the allegorical defence was the one most commonly advanced for poetic narrative. Nor was its application confined to poetry; it was extended to, or perhaps derived from, the myths which frequently underlay individual poems. Homer, Virgil, Ovid and Statius were treated as writers of allegory, and it is likely that the Roman poets at least wrote with an allegorical purpose consciously in mind.

Gilbert Murray remarked:

> All Hellenistic philosophy from the first Stoics onward is permeated by allegory. It is applied to Homer, to the religious traditions, to the whole world. To Sallustius after the end of our period the whole material world is only a great myth, a thing whose value lies not in itself but in the spiritual meaning which it hides and reveals. To Cleanthes at the beginning of it the universe was a mystic pageant, in which the immortal stars were the dancers and the Sun the priestly torch-bearer.

Chrysippus reduced the Homeric gods to physical or ethical principles; and Crates, the great critic, applied allegory in detail to his
interpretation of the all-wise poet. We possess two small but complete
treatises which illustrate well the results of this tendency, Cornutus
περὶ θεῶν ('About the Gods') and the *Homeric Allegories* of Heraclitus,
a brilliant little work of the first century B.C.

(*Five Stages of Greek Religion*, pp. 165–6)

Murray set much importance on the little-known work of
Sallustius, *About the Gods and the World*, which he translated as
an appendix to his *Five Stages*. Sallustius was in all probability a
friend of the emperor Julian (A.D. 332–63), whom he helped in his
attempt to reverse the Christian revolution of Julian's uncle,
the emperor Constantine I (A.D. 274–337). To illustrate the
developed form and doctrine of Graeco-Roman allegory, one
cannot do better than quote Chapters III and IV of Sallustius's
work:

III. *Concerning myths; that they are divine, and why.*

We may well inquire then, why the ancients forsook these doctrines
and made use of myths. There is this first benefit from myths, that we
have to search and do not have our mind idle.

That the myths are divine can be seen from those who have used
them. Myths have been used by inspired poets, by the best of philosophers, by those who established the mysteries, and by the Gods
themselves in oracles. But *why* the myths are divine it is the duty of
Philosophy to inquire. Since all existing things rejoice in that which
is like them and reject that which is unlike, the stories about the Gods
ought to be like the Gods, so that they may both be worthy of the
divine essence and make the Gods well disposed to those who speak
of them: which could only be done by means of myths.

Now the myths represent the Gods themselves and the goodness of
the Gods – subject always to the distinction of the speakable and the
unspeakable, the revealed and the unrevealed, that which is clear and
that which is hidden: since, just as the Gods have made the goods of
sense common to all, but those of intellect only to the wise, so the

myths state the existence of Gods to all, but who and what they are only to those who can understand.

They also represent the activities of the Gods. For one may call the World a Myth, in which bodies and things are visible, but souls and minds hidden. Besides, to wish to teach the whole truth about the Gods to all produces contempt in the foolish, because they cannot understand, and lack of zeal in the good; whereas to conceal the truth by myths prevents the contempt of the foolish, and compels the good to practise philosophy.

But why have they put in the myths stories of adultery, robbery, father-binding, and all the other absurdity? Is not that perhaps a thing worthy of admiration, done so that by means of the visible absurdity the Soul may immediately feel that the words are veils and believe the truth to be a mystery?

IV. *That the species of Myth are five, with examples of each.*

Of myths some are theological, some physical, some psychic, and again some material, and some mixed from these last two. The theological are those myths which use no bodily form but contemplate the very essences of the Gods: e.g. Kronos swallowing his children. Since God is intellectual, and all intellect returns into itself, this myth expresses in allegory the essence of God.

Myths may be regarded physically when they express the activities of the Gods in the world: e.g. people before now have regarded Kronos as Time, and calling the divisions of Time his sons say that the sons are swallowed by the father.

The psychic way is to regard the activities of the Soul itself: the Soul's acts of thought, though they pass on to other objects, nevertheless remain inside their begetters.

The material and last is that which the Egyptians have mostly used, owing to their ignorance, believing material objects actually to be Gods, and so calling them: e.g. they call the Earth Isis, moisture Osiris, heat Typhon, or again, water Kronos, the fruits of the earth Adonis, and wine Dionysus.

To say that these objects are sacred to the Gods, like various herbs and stones and animals, is possible to sensible men, but to say that they are gods is the notion of madmen – except, perhaps in the sense in which both the orb of the sun and the ray which comes from the orb are colloquially called 'the Sun'.

The mixed kind of myth may be seen in many instances: for example they say that in a banquet of the Gods Discord threw down a golden apple; the goddesses contended for it, and were sent by Zeus to Paris to be judged; Paris saw Aphrodite to be beautiful and gave her the apple. Here the banquet signifies the hyper-cosmic powers of the Gods; that is why they are all together. The golden apple is the world, which, being formed out of opposites, is naturally said to be 'thrown by Discord'. The different Gods bestow different gifts upon the world and are thus said to contend for the apple. And the soul which lives according to sense – for that is what Paris is – not seeing the other powers in the world but only beauty, declares that the apple belongs to Aphrodite.

Theological myths suit philosophers, physical and psychic suit poets, mixed suit religious initiations, since every initiation aims at uniting us with the World and the Gods.

To take another myth, they say that the Mother of the Gods seeing Attis lying by the river Gallus fell in love with him, took him, crowned him with her cap of stars, and thereafter kept him with her. He fell in love with a nymph and left the Mother to live with her. For this the Mother of the Gods made Attis go mad and cut off his genital organs and leave them with the Nymph, and then return and dwell with her.

Now the Mother of the Gods is the principle that generates life; that is why she is called Mother. Attis is the creator of all things which are born and die; that is why he is said to have been found by the river Gallus. For Gallus signifies the Galaxy, or Milky Way, the point at which body subject to passion begins. Now as the primary gods make perfect the secondary, the Mother loves Attis and gives him celestial powers. That is what the cap means. Attis loves a nymph: the nymphs preside over generation, since all that is generated is fluid. But since the process of generation must be stopped somewhere, and not allowed to generate something worse than the worst, the Creator who makes these things casts away his generative powers into the creation and is joined to the gods again. Now these things never happened, but always are. And Mind sees all things at once, but Reason (or Speech) expresses some first and other after. Thus, as the myth is in accord with the Cosmos, we for that reason keep a festival imitating the Cosmos, for how could we attain higher order?

And at first we ourselves, having fallen from heaven and living with the Nymph, are in despondence, and abstain from corn and all rich and unclean food, for both are hostile to the soul. Then comes the cutting of the tree and the fast, as though we also were cutting off the further process of generation. After that the feeding on milk, as though we were being born again; after which come rejoicings and garlands and, as it were, a return up to the Gods.

The season of the ritual is evidence to the truth of these explanations. The rites are performed about the Vernal Equinox, when the fruits of the earth are ceasing to be produced, and day is becoming longer than night, which applies well to Spirits rising higher. (At least, the other equinox is in mythology the time of the Rape of Korê, which is the descent of the souls.)

May these explanations of the myths find favour in the eyes of the Gods themselves and the souls of those who wrote the myths.

2
Biblical Allegory

The emphasis of chapter 1 fell especially on the different species of myth – narratives in which the plot may be analysed and interpreted at more than one level. Allegory of this kind we shall classify as narrative. Chapter 1 also contained examples of what may be called figural allegory. No myth, for instance, is attached to the figure of the goddess Natura; in herself she represents certain physical and intellectual qualities of the universe. Correspondingly, the structure of concentric spheres revealed to Er is itself an allegory of the moral government of the universe. The myth of Orpheus is narrative allegory, but in an isolated reference, the harp of Orpheus might be used as a figural allegory.

Allegories of both kinds are to be found in the Bible. St Paul's Ode to Charity (Corinthians XIII) is as much figural allegory as Aristotle's Ode to Virtue (*Oxford Book of Greek Verse*, pp. 469–70). So too Wisdom, as she is presented in Proverbs VIII is figural allegory. In some parables – those for instance of the Good Samaritan (Luke X, 30–35) and the Prodigal Son (Luke XV, 11–32) – the allegory is narrative.

Neither however is the most characteristic biblical form. During the present century, such scholars as Émile Mâle and G. R. Owst have revived interest in something different from either – typological allegory, a New Testament exegetic method which treats events and figures of the Old Testament as combining historical reality with prophetic meaning in terms of the Gospels and the Christian dispensation. The Old Testament events are 'types', figures, of events in the the New Testament. Typology dominated Christian thought and Christian art until the Reformation. Bede, for instance, defended it by reference to St Paul's declaration that all things happened to Israel in a figure, and were written for our admonition. The reference is to Corinthians X, 1–11. Here, as elsewhere, I quote the Authorized Version, save that in 6 and 11 I use the word 'types', to translate the Greek τύποι, 'types, figures' and τυπικῶς, 'in the manner of a type or figure':

> Moreover, brethren, I would not that ye should be ignorant, how that all our fathers were under the cloud, and all passed through the sea; and were all baptized unto Moses in the cloud and in the sea; and did all eat the same spiritual meat; and did all drink the same spiritual drink; for they drank of that spiritual Rock that followed them: and that Rock was Christ. But with many of them God was not well pleased: for they were overthrown in the wilderness. Now these things were our types, to the intent we should not lust after evil things as they also lusted. Neither be ye idolaters, as were some of them; as it is written, The people sat down to eat and drink, and rose up to play. Neither let us commit fornication, as some of them committed, and fell in one day three and twenty thousand. Neither let us tempt Christ, as some of them also tempted, and were destroyed of serpents. Neither murmur ye, as some of them also murmured, and were destroyed of the destroyer. Now all these things happened unto them for types: and they are written for our admonition, upon whom the ends of the world are come.

In this passage, Paul sees the exodus of the Children of Israel from Egypt as combining historical fact with a latent meaning which refers to the Christian Church. Egypt is the old life of sin; the Promised Land is the Kingdom of God; the wilderness is the struggle for salvation during this life. The miraculous crossing of the Red Sea together with the subsequent guidance by the pillar of cloud corresponds to Christian baptism; manna corresponds to the bread of the Eucharist; the water which sprang from the Rock corresponds to the wine of the Eucharist; Moses and the Rock correspond to Christ, and there may also be a reference to Peter, the Rock on which Christ built his church. Equally however the sins and failings of the Children of Israel correspond to sins and failings in the young Christian church at Corinth and, by implication, elsewhere. The Old Testament events stand to the New Testament ones as types, τύποι, a word which in Greek has as its basic meaning, 'something struck out; a print, impression of a seal'. The seal is the New Testament event, which has struck out a prophetic impression of itself in the pages of the Old Testament. In terms of temporal logic, the process seems impossible, but in terms of the dynamics of eternity, no particular difficulty is involved.

Among many other examples, one might quote the interpretation which allegorizes the Song of Solomon in terms of the mutual love of Christ and the Church. Solomon is a type of Christ, the Queen of Sheba represents the Church, and New Testament authority for the interpretation is to be found in Matthew XII, 42:

> The queen of the south shall rise up in the judgement with this generation, and shall condemn it: for she came from the uttermost parts of the earth to hear the wisdom of Solomon; and, behold, a greater than Solomon is here.

A clearer example is to be found in Galatians IV, 22–9:

> Abraham had two sons, the one by a bondmaid, the other by a freewoman. But he who was of the bondwoman was born after the flesh; but he of the freewoman was by promise. Which things are an allegory: for these are the two covenants; the one from the mount Sinai, which gendereth to bondage, which is Agar. For this Agar is mount Sinai in Arabia, and answereth to Jerusalem which now is, and is in bondage with her children. But Jerusalem which is above is free, which is the mother of us all. For it is written, Rejoice, thou barren that bearest not; break forth and cry, thou that travailest not: for the desolate hath many more children than she which hath an husband.
>
> Now we, brethren, as Isaac was, are the children of promise. But as then he that was born after the flesh persecuted him that was born after the spirit, even so it is now.

'St. Paul wrote this letter to his Galatian converts on receiving news of a counter-mission requiring them to keep all the commands of the Jewish Law' (*Oxford Dictionary of the Christian Church*, sv. 'Galatians'). He felt passionately that Gentile Christians were not required to accept all the Mosaic enactments – that the Law of Moses had been superseded by the new Christian Law of Freedom. The process he illustrated by the history of Abraham's two sons, the elder, Ishmael, who was the son of the bondwoman, Hagar (Agar), and the younger, Isaac, the son of promise, who was miraculously born to Abraham's wife, Sarah, when she was ninety years old and Abraham one hundred (Genesis XVI, XVII, XXI). Hagar, Paul says, is a type of Mount Sinai, where Moses later received the Old Law, and so of the Jerusalem of his own day, the site of the Jewish Temple, and the centre of the Jewish people and religion. Sarah is a type of the Heavenly Jerusalem of the Christian Church. The miraculous birth of Isaac typifies the virgin birth of Christ, as is further illustrated by the messianic quotation from Deutero-Isaiah (Isaiah LIV, 1).

Paul's attitude is not unique in the New Testament. In Matthew XII, 40–2, for instance, we read:

> As Jonas was three days and three nights in the whale's belly; so shall the Son of Man be three days and three nights in the heart of the earth.

Jonah in the whale's belly is an allegory of the Descent into Hell and Resurrection of Christ during the period from Good Friday to Easter Day. A more complicated example is to be found in John III, 14–15:

> And as Moses lifted up the serpent in the wilderness, even so must the Son of man be lifted up: that whosoever believeth in him should not perish, but have everlasting life.

The Old Testament incident which John interprets as a type of salvation by the Cross is to be found in Numbers XXI, 5–9:

And the people spake against God, and against Moses, Wherefore
have ye brought us up out of Egypt to die in the wilderness? for there
is no bread, neither is there any water; and our soul loatheth this light
bread. And the Lord sent fiery serpents among the people, and they
bit the people; and much people of Israel died. Therefore the people
came to Moses, and said. We have sinned, for we have spoken against
the Lord, and against thee; pray unto the Lord, that he take away the
serpents from us. And Moses prayed for the people. And the Lord said
unto Moses, Make thee a fiery serpent, and set it upon a pole: and it
shall come to pass, that every one that is bitten, when he looketh upon
it shall live. And Moses made a serpent of brass, and put it upon a pole,
and it came to pass, that if a serpent had bitten any man, when he
beheld the serpent of brass, he lived.

The main Old Testament personages who typify aspects of the
New Testament – 'so great a cloud of witnesses' – are listed in
Hebrews XI. They are Abel, Enoch, Noah, Abraham, Isaac, Jacob,
Joseph, Moses, Rahab, Gideon, Barak, Samson, Jephthah, David,
Samuel and the Prophets. In this list we have a stage in the development of a new point of view. In full Christian form, this saw history, not as sequence, but as process, directed from Creation and
the Fall of Man towards the Incarnation and Redemption, and
finally to Judgement Day. The ultimately significant events were
concentrated into the few years of the earthly life of Jesus, the
carpenter's son from Nazareth. All history had become a typology,
whose meaning was to be assessed in terms of a single humble life
which had apparently ended in ignominy.

This Christian view, however, was the consummation of the
earlier Jewish idea of Israel as God's kingdom, eventually to be led
by Messiah to the peaceful government of the world. The Christian
view was more inner-directed, in a sense more humble, and much
closer to life as it was lived in the Mediterranean world of the
Roman Empire and afterwards. The best analysis of the way in
which this new point of view affected literature is to be found in
Erich Auerbach's *Mimesis*.

Typological allegory forms an important subdivision of the more general prophetic and situational allegory, which is characteristic of Old and New Testament alike. The allegorical force of the four instances of typology discussed above – the Song of Solomon, Ishmael and Isaac, Jonah and the Whale, the Serpent in the Wilderness – depends not so much on a story, a narrative, as on a situation: mutual love; the difference in birth which separated the half-brothers; the plight of Jonah rather than the circumstances which brought him into that plight; the miraculous healing of the Israelites by an image of the serpent which had poisoned them. The full meaning becomes apparent in terms only of the future. A figure may be involved, but to bring out the allegorical meaning, it stands, not in isolation, but in a meaningful context. The prophetic situation rather than the figure forms the allegory. Narrative is not involved, or if it is, it is at a fairly rudimentary level. If we return for comparison to the biblical examples already quoted, the typological allegories include no narrative complications, such as the introduction of the priest and Levite in the parable of the Good Samaritan, or the behaviour of the elder brother in that of the Prodigal Son. The relationship of prophetic and situational to narrative allegory resembles that of dramatic monologue to drama.

The majority of the New Testament parables are examples of prophetic and situational allegory, not involving typology. To illustrate, one may use the parable generally known as that of the Sower, but which might better be called The Seeds and the Ground. I quote the earliest extant version, that in Mark IV, 3–8. Very similar versions, perhaps derived from this, are to be found in Matthew XIII, 3–8 and Luke VIII, 5–8:

Behold, there went out a sower to sow: and it came to pass, as he sowed, some fell by the wayside, and the fowls of the air came and devoured it up. And some fell on stony ground, where it had not much earth; and immediately it sprung up, because it had no depth of earth: but when the sun was up, it was scorched; and because it had no root, it withered away. And some fell among thorns, and the thorns grew up, and choked it, and it yielded no fruit. And other fell on good ground, and did yield fruit that sprang up and increased; and brought forth, some thirty, and some sixty, and some an hundred.

The parable is thus interpreted by Mark (IV, 14–20), as by Matthew (XIII, 19–23) and Luke (VIII, 11–15):

The sower soweth the word. And these are they by the wayside, where the word is sown; but when they have heard, Satan cometh immediately, and taketh away the word that was sown in their hearts. And these are they likewise which are sown on stony ground; who, when they have heard the word, immediately receive it with gladness; and have no root in themselves, and so endure but for a time: afterward, when affliction or persecution ariseth for the world's sake, immediately they are offended. And these are they which are sown among thorns; such as hear the word, and the cares of this world, and the deceitfulness of riches, and the lusts of other things entering in, choke the word, and it becometh unfruitful. And these are they which are sown on good ground; such as hear the word, and receive it, and bring forth fruit, some thirty-fold, some sixty, and some an hundred.

During the present century, this interpretation, despite its high scriptural warranty, has met with some adverse criticism. C. H. Dodd, for instance, remarks:

The seed is the Word: yet the crop which comes up is composed of various classes of people . . . Two inconsistent lines of interpretation have been mixed up.

(*The Parables of the Kingdom*, p. 15)

Dodd, I feel, has allowed himself to slip into error because he saw the parable as figural, with the seed as figure, rather than situational, with the inter-relationship of seed and ground giving rise to the allegory. The Gospel interpretation contains some verbal clumsiness, but it is perfectly clear that conceptually seed and ground remain separate; that the different kinds of ground (*not* seed) represent different kinds of human being, and that the crop, or lack of it, results from different kinds of interaction between ground and seed. The seed, in other words, represents a divine addition to the raw material of humanity, which under certain conditions may produce something neither seed nor ground, but transcending both. Dodd's suggestion – 'The wayside and the birds, the thorns and the stony ground are not, as Mark supposed, cryptograms for persecution, the deceitfulness of riches, and so forth. They are there to conjure up a picture of the vast amount of wasted labour which the farmer must face, and so to bring into relief the satisfaction that the harvest gives, in spite of all' (p. 19) – is inadequate, partly because Dodd mistakenly equates allegory with cryptogram, partly because he does not consider the parable as situation. Some sophistication in the way of references to persecution may have crept in, but basically Mark's interpretation is sound.

A further problem is the meaning to be attached to the fruit, the harvest produced from the good ground. In Mark IV, as in Matthew XIII, several parables occur, of which all the others refer to the transcendental doctrine of the Kingdom. Many are introduced by some variant of the phrase, 'So is the Kingdom of God, as if . . .' Perhaps the most apposite is the parable of the Seed Growing Secretly (Mark IV, 26–9):

> So is the kingdom of God, as if a man should cast seed into the ground; and should sleep, and rise night and day, and the seed should spring and grow up, he knoweth not how. For the earth bringeth forth fruit of herself; first the blade, then the ear, after that the full corn in the ear. But when the fruit is brought forth, immediately he putteth in the sickle, because the harvest is come.

The allegory is also situational – it is indeed a straightforward enough variation on the Seeds and the Ground – but it differs in that it makes it clear that the reaping of the harvest represents the advent of the Kingdom of God. Beyond this point of interpretation it is not necessary for the literary theorist to pursue the meaning.

The establishment of the Kingdom of God, however, was the immediate concern of Christ and the early Christians, and this introduces another fact of great importance. In Chapter 1, I emphasized that much classical myth and allegory dealt with the day-to-day or year-to-year routine of life. Its success partly resulted from the fact that figural or narrative allegory to some extent distanced, and so made comprehensible and controllable, the events with which they dealt. The situational allegory of the Bible is on the whole more direct and immediate. The New Testament parables were told to an audience which realized, as it listened, that the Kingdom was there and then coming into existence, or was already fully present. For such an audience, the parables were more relevant, more exciting, than even the latest political or military news. This is as true of the apparently narrative or figural allegories as of the situational.

All New Testament allegory, and in particular all New Testament situational allegory, originated from a feeling that author and audience alike were participating in a new and extraordinary situation. The feeling is especially acute in the New Testament, but by no means confined to it. To a considerable extent, the first Christians acquired the sense of participation from their Jewish ancestors and contemporaries, for whom, no matter how black the immediate future might seem, the eventual establishment of Israel, God's people, as God's kingdom, had remained self-evident and all-important. The transformation of Israel to the Christian church, and the consequent parallel and opposition of the new and old Israels, is to be seen throughout Paul's Epistle to the Galatians, and especially at the close (VI, 16–17):

> For in Christ Jesus neither circumcision availeth any thing, nor uncircumcision, but a new creature. And as many as walk according to this rule, peace be on them, and mercy, and upon the Israel of God.

From his standpoint in time Paul saw the old Israel as a type of the new Kingdom, and one proof that his sense of continuity did not fail him is to be found in the fact that the Old Testament – in particular, the later books of the Old Testament – is as full of prophetic situational allegory as the New.

Isaiah V, 1–7, will serve as an example:

> My wellbeloved hath a vineyard in a very fruitful hill: and he fenced it, and gathered out the stones thereof, and planted it with the choicest vine, and built a tower in the midst of it, and also made a wine-press therein: and he looked that it should bring forth grapes, and it brought forth wild grapes.
>
> 'And now, O inhabitants of Jerusalem, and men of Judah, judge, I pray you, betwixt me and my vineyard. What could have been done more to my vineyard, that I have not done in it? wherefore, when I looked that it should bring forth grapes, brought it forth wild grapes?
>
> And now go to; I will tell you what I will do to my vineyard: I will take away the hedge thereof, and it shall be eaten up; and break down the wall thereof, and it shall be trodden down: and I will lay it waste: it shall not be pruned, nor digged; but there shall come up briers and thorns: I will also command the clouds that they rain no rain upon it.'
>
> For the vineyard of the Lord of hosts is the house of Israel, and the men of Judah his pleasant plant: and he looked for judgment, but behold oppression; for righteousness, but behold a cry.

The interpretation given in the final paragraph makes it plain that the allegory is to be interpreted in terms of the political and social realities of Isaiah's own time, the eighth century B.C. The vineyard is Palestine as a whole, the area occupied by the two kingdoms of Israel and Judah. The vine is the kingdom and royal house of Judah: the tower perhaps Jerusalem. The wild grapes represent both the oppression inflicted by the rulers of Judah on their people, and the cries of the oppressed. It is scarcely too much to say that here allegory has become the instrument for satire, even political satire – satire, too, which is the more effective for the imaginative vigour of the image in which it is embodied. For the people of a Mediterranean country, the vine in the vineyard represents at once

c

the fruitfulness of the plant, the orderliness of the society which enabled the landowner to build and maintain the vineyard, the promise of the vintage, and equally the possibility of disappointed expectations. One may compare the varied use of the same image in Psalm LXXX, 8–17 and John XV, 1–8.

A similar use of situational allegory for satire, or at least attack on external enemies is to be found in *Ezekiel* XXVII – XXXII. The passage was probably written in the sixth century B.C.. Tyre is presented as a magnificent merchant ship, wrecked at sea:

> The rowers have brought thee into great waters; the east wind hath broken thee in the midst of the seas.

[XXVIII, 26]

(The east wind is Nebuchadnezzar, who captured Jerusalem in 586 B.C.). The Egyptian Pharaoh is the Nile crocodile, hooked and thrown out to rot on the desert:

> Thus saith the Lord God: Behold, I am against thee, Pharaoh king of Egypt, the great dragon that lieth in the midst of his rivers, which hath said, My river is mine own, and I have made it for myself. But I will put hooks in thy jaws, and I will cause the fish of thy rivers to stick unto thy scales, and I will bring thee up out of the midst of thy rivers, and all the fish of thy rivers shall stick unto thy scales. And I will leave thee thrown into the wilderness, thee and all the fish of thy rivers: thou shalt fall upon the open fields; thou shalt not be brought together, nor gathered: I have given thee for meat to the beasts of the field and to the fowls of heaven.

(XXIX, 3–5)

Merchant ship and crocodile are obviously appropriate emblems for Tyre and Egypt. An emblem however is static: Ezekiel transformed them into situational allegories by prophesying the wreck of the ship, the ignominious destruction of the crocodile – both future events in God's providential scheme for the world.

It is this overwhelming concern with the divinely operated movement of history which, more than anything else, distinguished biblical from classical allegory, and which made it so potent an instrument for the later European literatures. The Roman poet Horace (65–8 B.C.) also made use of allegory for purposes of satire, but a comparison of the sixth satire of his second book will show how far he fell short of the power and range of the Old Testament prophets. However general the possible applications, his immediate purpose remained personal:

> O rus, quando ego te aspiciam? quandoque licebit
> nunc veterum libris, nunc somno et inertibus horis
> ducere sollicitae iucunda oblivia vitae?

(60–2)

(Countryside, when shall I see you? And when shall I be allowed to enjoy sweet forgetfulness of the cares of life, now among the books of the ancients, now in sleep and hours of relaxation?)

His attitude is summarized by the Aesopic fable of the country mouse who, to his sorrow, visited his friend in town. The mere fact that the illustrative allegory is a story of two mice frightened by dogs helps to maintain the detached, gentlemanly, humorous level at which Horace's satire operates. In this poem, allegory and prophecy, satire and the history and purpose of the world, have nothing in common.

This observation at least partially fails with some others among Horace's poems. Quintilian, for instance, the Roman critic who lived from A.D. 35–95, illustrates his definition of allegory (*Institutio Oratoria* VIII, vi, 44) by a reference to Horace *Odes* I, xiv, *O navis, referent in mare*. Quintilian comments, *navem pro re publica, fluctus et tempestates pro bellis civilibus, portum pro pace atque concordia dicit*, 'by ship he intends the state, by waves and winds the civil wars, by the harbour peace and tranquillity' – a convincing interpretation, which shows Horace's poetic involvement at least with immediate political circumstances, and which also brings out the parallel with Ezekiel's treatment of Tyre under the image of a ship. It also emphasizes the great difference between the two authors and the cultures which produced them. Horace's allegory tends towards the figural rather than the situational. The image of the ship is capable of much more dramatic development in terms of the city of the sea-faring Phoenicians than of the land-based might of Rome. For Horace, too, the image is a commonplace, directly or indirectly derived from 'Ασυννέτημι τὼν ἀνέμων στάσιν ('I fail to understand the strife of the winds', *Oxford Book of Greek Verse*, pp. 167–8), a political lyric by the Greek poet Alcaeus (c. 600 B.C.). This commonplace Horace develops with taste and skill, but for Ezekiel the image is part of a living reality. Horace, finally, sees the situation in terms of human prudence and foresight: Ezekiel sees God shaping the world to his purposes.

Virgil, in the *Aeneid* and the fourth *Eclogue*, was capable of seeing the divine purpose at work in a long series of historical events, but in the world of Greece and Rome Virgil is a unique figure, in some ways more akin to the spirituality of the Middle Ages than to the philosophy of his contemporaries. Even Virgil's sense of purpose in history, however, seems colourless in comparison with that of the last scriptural author to be discussed, John, who at the end of the first century A.D. wrote Revelation, the concluding book of the New Testament. All modern scholarship seems to be in agreement that this book deals allegorically with events of the period, in particular the persecution of Christians by the Roman emperors Nero (54–68 A.D.) and Domitian (81–96 A.D.), and with the expectation of the return of Christ to earth in judgement. John was concerned not merely with history, but the consummation of history which he believed himself to be witnessing.

John's book is a connected series of visions, any one of which – for instance, the woman clothed with the sun, travailing in birth (XII, 1–2) – might properly be regarded as situational allegory. Typology is everywhere taken for granted. All this is in the normal biblical tradition. Structurally however the book makes use of a style of allegory which, although it might easily be paralleled elsewhere, has not yet been discussed in this essay. I mean alphabetic and numerical allegory.

The entire book revolves on the phrase which in the first and last chapters John placed in the mouth of Christ, 'I am Alpha and Omega, the first and the last' (I, 11: cf. XXI, 6 and XXII, 13). Alpha and omega (α and ω) are the first and last letters of the Greek alphabet, to which Revelation bears no structural correspondence. It is important however to notice that the book contains twenty-two chapters, and that in the Hebrew as opposed to the Greek alphabet, there are twenty-two letters. The Hebrew alphabet had in the past been used to impose form on shorter Old Testament writings; the so-called Acrostic Psalms, for instance, of which the best known is Psalm CXIX with its twenty-two alphabetic divisions, and also the series of elegies on the fall of Jerusalem in 586 B.C. which form the individual chapters of the Lamentations of Jeremiah. The first and second of those each contains twenty-two three-line stanzas, the fourth, twenty-two two-line stanzas, and in each elegy every stanza begins with the appropriate letter of the Hebrew alphabet in sequence. Chapter III has sixty-six lines, arranged in triplets, the lines of which begin aaa; bbb, etc. Chapter V has twenty-two lines, but no acrostic.

Although those alphabetic patterns were certainly intended to be meaningful, today it is not always possible to find their exact significance. If we assume that John deliberately adopted a similar pattern for Revelation, the significance is easier to grasp. Form and content are very closely related. The content is the history of the world, seen in the context of Christ's statement that he is Alpha and Omega, the first and last letters of the alphabet. The twenty-two chapters, in which the history of the world finds formai expression, correspond to the twenty-two letters of the Hebrew alphabet, which is also that of the history written by God in the book sealed with seven seals (V.1). Naturally enough in a work composed during the Domitianic persecution, the emphasis falls more on the last than on the first stages of the entire process.

Alphabetic merges easily into numerical imagery. The creation of the world occupied six of the seven days of the first week, and already in books of the New Testament other than *Revelation* one finds traces of the opinion, which soon became universal, that the history of the world was to occupy six ages, corresponding to the six days of creation, and followed by the sabbath of eternal rest. The genealogy of Christ in Matthew I traces, with some artificiality explained below, his descent from Abraham through three series of fourteen generations: from Christ to the Babylonian Captivity; from the Captivity to David; from David to Abraham. The very different genealogy in Luke III, 23–38 carries the line by way of Noah and Adam back to creation. The birth of Christ was regarded by all Christians as the beginning of a new age, which was to be concluded by the Second Coming. In those gospels we already have in embryonic form the Seven Ages of the World: the first from Adam to Noah; the second from Noah to Abraham; the third from Abraham to David; the fourth from David to the Captivity; the fifth from the Captivity to the birth of Christ; the sixth from Christ to Judgement; the seventh the eternity which follows Judgement. Matthew lays particular emphasis on the distinctively Jewish portion of the history, from Abraham to Christ; this occupies forty-two generations, or six 'days' each consisting of a 'week' of seven generations. The sabbath of this week of weeks began with the birth of Christ.

Seven is the sum of four and three. The first four days of Genesis I saw the creation of the inanimate universe: on the first day light and darkness; on the second, the separation of the waters above from those below the firmament; on the third, the separation of land and sea, and the creation of vegetation; on the fourth, the creation of sun, moon and stars. The remaining three days saw the

animate creation, including that of human beings, and the establishment of the day of rest, which has meaning in terms only of the
animate creation and of God. On the fourth day, 'signs and seasons, days and years' were established in conjunction with the
creation of sun, moon and stars. All those may be seen in terms of
seven, its two component parts, four and three, the product of four
and three, twelve, and twice twelve, twenty-four. The seven days
of the week are to be connected with the seven planets readily
visible to the naked eye; the months of four weeks is connected
with the complete series of phases of the moon; the apparent movement of the sun through the twelve signs of the stellar zodiac
establishes the year of twelve months. The four seasons each
occupy three months of the year. The day is divided primarily into
two, secondly into twenty-four parts, the twelve inequal hours of
day and night respectively. Twelve also played a dominating part
in the movement of history. In particular, there were the twelve
tribes of old Israel, and the twelve apostles whose authority for the
new Israel Christ himself had established. Two, three, four, seven,
twelve and twenty-four are the numbers which have a particularly
powerful allegorical meaning in relation to time and history.

In conjunction with the alphabetic framework, those numbers
establish the structure and much of the meaning of Revelation.
Seven is the most obviously important. Shailer Matthews for
instance, in the article on Revelation in Hastings' *Dictionary of the
Bible*, made an analysis of the book into seven main components.
Not all scholars would agree with the analysis, but the general
importance of seven cannot be denied. To select only the most
conspicuous examples, the main action of the book begins with the
letters to the seven churches (chapters II and III), where as G. B.
Caird points out in his commentary (pp. 14–15), 'John uses the
number seven as a symbol for completeness or wholeness . . . .
There were more churches in the Roman province of Asia than he
names . . . John chooses seven of the churches to indicate that his

message is really addressed to the church at large.' (The church at large, one should remember, is the Israel of God.) Chapters V–VIII are occupied with the breaking of the seals to open 'a book written within and on the backside, sealed with seven seals' (V, 1). This book Caird interprets (p. 72) as 'the world's destiny, fore-ordained by the gracious purpose of God'. The seven seals opened by the Lamb have a fairly obvious connection with the seven days of creation and the seven ages of the world. The opening is followed by the blowing of seven trumpets (VIII–XI) and the pouring out of seven vials (XV–XVI). After the opening of the seventh seal, 'there was silence in heaven about the space of half an hour' (VIII, 1). After the sounding of the seventh trumpet, 'there were great voices in heaven, saying, The kingdoms of this world are become the kingdoms of our Lord, and of his Christ; and he shall reign for ever and ever' (XI, 15). After the pouring of the seventh vial, 'there came a great voice out of the temple of heaven, from the throne, saying, It is done' (VI, 17). The three series of sevens, all this is probably to say, are not to be taken as occurring in strict temporal succession; each represents a process which comes to a conclusion only at the end of the world.

As in *Genesis* I, two of those three groups of seven tend to fall into subdivisions of four and three. This is most obvious with the seven seals. The Four Horsemen of the Apocalypse appear as the first four seals are opened, and the appearance of each is proclaimed by one of the four beasts who stand around the throne of Christ. 'And the first beast was like a lion, and the second beast like a calf, and the third beast had a face as a man, and the fourth beast was like a flying eagle' (IV, 7; cf. Ezekiel I, 10). In view of their proximity to Christ, the beasts were afterwards identified with the four evangelists, Mark, Luke, Matthew and John respectively. By contrast, John places greater emphasis on the sounding of the last three than on that of the first four trumpets, and throughout this episode the fraction one-third is often repeated. The first trumpet

destroys one third of the trees on earth; the second turns one third
of the sea to blood; the third destroys one third of the rivers; the
fourth destroys one third of the sun, the moon and the stars: at the
sixth, four angels destroy one third of the human race by fire,
smoke and brimstone. Those trumpets in fact destroy one third of
the work of the four latter days of creation.

Twelve, the product of four and three, is most conspicuous in
connection with the bride of the Lamb, New Jerusalem (XXI–
XXII). The city has twelve gates, three in each of the four walls,
and each gate is named for one of the twelve tribes of Israel. It has
twelve foundations, each named after one of the twelve apostles.
In form, the city is a cube, with a length and breadth and height of
twelve thousand furlongs (1,500 miles!). The height of the wall, as
opposed perhaps to the height of the city, is 144 cubits (144 = 12 x
12; cf. the 144,000 who in VII are sealed), but it is worth noticing
that the cubits are to be measured in terms of the arm of an angel
(XXI, 17); 144 angelic cubits may be equivalent to twelve thousand
earthly furlongs. The precious stones which make up the twelve
foundations are those which were believed to have a mystic correspondence with the twelve signs of the Zodiac, but, for whatever
reason, John places them in an order precisely the reverse of that
usually found in astrological records. Within the city grows the
Tree of Life, 'which bare twelve manner of fruits, and yielded her
fruit every month: and the leaves of the tree were for the healing
of the nations' (XXII, 2).

Twenty-four is most conspicuous in the description of the
heavenly throne and its setting, which forms chapter IV. Twenty-
four elders are seated about the throne, and each of the four beasts,
who are also present, has six wings. The figure twenty-four may,
I suggest, represent the sum of the hours of the day, which, like
that of the days of the week, on occasions represents the completed
course of time.

Duality is found throughout the book, most notably perhaps in such oppositions as that of Beast and Lamb, or of the two cities, Babylon the harlot, and New Jerusalem the bride of the Lamb. The temporal parallel is the opposition of day and night, which in turn corresponds spiritually to the opposition of good and evil. The duality disappears with the final establishment of New Jerusalem:

> And the city had no need of the sun, neither of the moon, to shine in it: for the glory of God did lighten it, and the Lamb is the light thereof. And the nations of them which are saved shall walk in the light of it: and the kings of the earth do bring their glory and honour into it. And the gates of it shall not be shut at all by day: for there shall be no night there.
>
> (XXI, 23–5)

3
Allegory and the Course of Time

As the Christian community expanded, it did not lose the sense which it had inherited of history as purposeful allegory. This sense, for instance helps to reconcile Bede, the historian who in 731 A.D. produced the critical and factual *Ecclesiastical History of the English Nation*, with Bede, the biblical commentator who believed that 'All things in Scripture – times and places, names and numbers, are full of spiritual figure, of typic mystery, of heavenly sacraments' (C. Plummer, *Baedae Opera Historica* I, lvi). For Bede, as for later medieval historians, the source of all historical movement was the providential purpose of God, operating within the framework of the six ages during which the work of the six days of creation was to endure.

Well before Bede's time, the geographical extension of the Christian community, and the fact that the great majority of Christians were also Gentiles, had led to considerable alteration of emphasis in the originally Jewish concept. In the period which preceded the Babylonian Captivity – before, that is to say, 586 B.C. – the Jews had regarded themselves as the chosen people, in sole terms of whom the divine purpose had and would operate in history. The existence of Gentile powers and kingdoms seemed relatively unimportant. The Babylonian Captivity and the consequent Jewish diaspora began the change which the life of Christ and the work of the Apostles completed, a change the beginning of which is already apparent in the Old Testament book of Daniel, written about 165 B.C. In this, Gentile rulers – Nebuchadnezzar,

Darius and Cyrus – are presented with some sympathy; they are major instruments moreover in furthering the divine purpose, and are represented as becoming in some sense converts to the God of Daniel. This of itself was important to the Church in the early phase of mission to, and persecution by, the Roman Empire. The conversion of the Emperor Constantine in 312 A.D. appeared almost to complete the process whose beginnings Daniel was believed to have described.

Even more important was the prophetic element in the book, and in particular the interpretation by Daniel of Nebuchadnezzar's first dream, that of the statue, the head of which was golden, the breast and arms silver, the belly and thighs brass, the legs iron, and the feet partly iron and partly clay. The statue was destroyed by a stone:

> Thou sawest till that a stone was cut out without hands, which smote the image upon his feet that were of iron and clay, and brake them to pieces. Then was the iron, the clay, the brass, the silver, and the gold, broken to pieces together, and became like the chaff of the summer threshing-floors; and the wind carried them away, that no place was found for them: and the stone that smote the image became a great mountain, and filled the whole earth.

> (Daniel II, 34–5)

Daniel interpreted this prophetic situational allegory in terms of four kingdoms, the last of which was to suffer division, and eventually to be superseded by the stone, the eternal Kingdom of God. For an orthodox medieval Christian only one meaning was possible. The golden head was the Babylonian Empire; the silver breast and arms the Persian Empire; the brass belly and thighs the Macedonian Empire of Alexander the Great; the iron legs the Roman Empire; and the feet of iron and clay the European kingdoms and principalities with which he was himself familiar. The stone was the constantly expected coming of Christ in judgement.

The fulfilment of God's purpose thus involved the rise and fall of secular empires, each inferior to the one which preceded, a process which became known as the *translatio imperii* or 'transfer of Empire'. The continuing existence of secular powers, separate from and yet involved in the spiritual development represented by the old and new Israels, came to be represented in practical terms by the contrasted offices of Holy Roman Emperor and Pope. Empire in the restrictive sense of Nebuchadnezzar's dream, was limited to the fifth and sixth ages of the world. The ground however had been prepared in the second age of the world when God first brought separate nations and languages into existence at the destruction of the Tower of Babel (Genesis XI, 1–9). All non-biblical history necessarily belonged to a period subsequent to this event. Virtually all non-biblical history, on the other hand, might be regarded as contributing to the rise or fall of one of the four Empires, or to the nation states of medieval Europe.

Eusebius, bishop of Caesarea (c. A.D. 260–340) imposed some kind of literary form on this allegorical concept. His *World-Chronicle* was arranged in parallel vertical columns, one of which devoted to each of the nations whose total history he proposed to illustrate. Dates, estimated from the Creation in terms of the ages of the world were indicated along the edge in such a way that, for a reader to find what had happened anywhere at a given time, it was only necessary to locate the date and glance across the vertical columns. The *World-Chronicle* was translated into Latin and continued by St Jerome (c. A.D. 342–420). Thereafter it was further expanded and continued by Prosper of Aquitaine (c. A.D. 390–463) in his *Chronicle,* and by Isidore of Seville in his *Chronica Majora.*

Bede, who was thoroughly familiar with Isidore's writings, found them particularly useful for his work on chronology, work necessitated by the Easter controversy which during his time still divided parts of the Celtic church in Britain from the Roman tradition. In this field, his main works were the short *De Temporibus* (A.D. 703) and the *De Temporum Ratione* (A.D. 725). Each concluded with a world-chronicle, based ultimately on Eusebius. The brief entries in *De Temporibus* contain almost nothing about affairs in England, or indeed in the British Isles. Many entries on English affairs appear in the longer and more detailed chronicle which concludes *De Temporum Ratione*. It is fairly obvious that the labour which Bede devoted to harmonizing English with world history for *De Temporum Ratione* helped to prepare him for work on the *Ecclesiastical History*, and that in the latter work one at least of his motives was to show the contribution of the English to the providential scheme for the sixth age of the world. Even so painstaking and scholarly a work, in other words, had a function which was at least partly allegorical, and a place in a scheme which was entirely allegorical.

The importance of allegory for world-history is most readily apparent in fields other than that of the pure historian. Émile Mâle, for instance, has shown how medieval painting, sculpture and stained glass served to illustrate the allegorical concept of history. In effect, a medieval church of any size was a historical allegory written in stone, glass and wood. It is quite wrong to think of allegory as necessarily verbal; throughout the Middle Ages and Renaissance the visual as well as the verbal arts became vehicles for allegory, both biblical and classical. The visual arts lie outside the compass of this book, but the subject is important, and the reader who wishes to pursue the matter should begin by consulting Mâle or Seznec's *The Survival of the Pagan Gods*.

To some extent activities within and around the church corresponded to the plan and decoration of the building itself. Here the observance of the Christian Year became a matter of the first importance. Christ had suffered, not merely under Pontius Pilate, but at a precise time of year, established in terms of the Jewish Passover, the date of which was in turn established by the phases of the moon in relation to the Vernal Equinox (21st March). From the beginning, the Christian community commemorated the

Passion and Resurrection within the few weeks which followed the Vernal Equinox. From the fourth century onwards, the Western Church celebrated the Birth of Christ on 25th December. The dates of other major fasts and festivals largely depended on those two major commemorations. Lent, Ascension, Whit, Trinity and Corpus Christi, for instance, depended on the moveable Easter; Advent, Childermas (28th December), Epiphany (6th January), Candlemas (2nd February), Lady Day (25th March), and St John Baptist (24th June), on the immovable Christmas.

As the major commemorations became established, so the form of worship in the churches adopted a more or less fixed form, which generally came to include readings from the Old as well as the New Testament. It was natural to include the appropriate prophetic and typological passages from the Old Testament as part of the service at major festivals. New Testament and Old Testament narratives alike often contained a highly dramatic element, which gradually asserted itself, a process, the eventual result of which was the cyclical miracle plays of medieval Western Europe. The overall subject-matter of the cycles was the allegorical history of the world from Creation to Judgement. Old Testament events were selected for inclusion insofar as they were types of events in the New Testament. Events after the Crucifixion were drawn partly from the New Testament, partly from such apocryphal narratives as the *Gospel of Nicodemus* and the *Assumption of the Virgin* (both of which may bè consulted in M. R. James, *The Apocryphal New Testament*, Oxford, 1924).

Bede, as historian, had been concerned with the obverse of Old Testament typology – that is to say, with a retrospective typology which put the events of his own time and country into the providential scheme centring on the Crucifixion and Resurrection. He was too good a historian to attempt to trace the history of the English people to a period anterior to the sixth age. Others were less scrupulous. In particular, the synthetic historians of Ireland

and Wales concocted elaborate narrative links between themselves and the events of remote periods. The most successful was Geoffrey of Monmouth (c. 1100–55), whose *History of the Kings of Britain*, completed c. 1135, set out a long and (for the most part) fictitious line of British kings, beginning with Brutus, great-grandson of Aeneas, who came to the throne at a time when Eli the priest ruled in Judea, and the Ark of the Covenant had been captured by the Philistines; when the sons of Hector ruled in Troy after the expulsion of the descendants of Antenor, and when Silvius Aeneas ruled in Italy. (The Eusebian framework shows clearly in this method of dating.) The line ended with Cadwaladr, who died, according to Geoffrey, in A.D. 689. The most famous king in the sequence was Arthur. In Geoffrey's work, the providential scheme is clearly visible. The Britons almost attain Empire when Arthur defeats and kills the Roman emperor, Lucius. The design is frustrated by the sinfulness and contumely of Arthur's fellow-Britons, more particularly that of his nephew Modred, and from the heights the Britons descend to the humiliation of the Anglo-Saxon conquest. This last was a divine judgement, but as such it formed part of the providential scheme revealed to Cadwaladr when he was about to mount an expedition to recover his lost fortunes. An angel warned him to desist:

> For God was unwilling that the Britons should rule any longer in the island of Britain before the time had come which Merlin has prophesied to Arthur . . . He said also that the Britons would in the future obtain the island as a reward for their faith, after the fatal time had elapsed.
>
> (XII, xviii)

It sounds very much as if the Britons were not to recover the island until the millenium or the Day of Judgement.

For the medieval European imagination, temporal power and magnificence came to be represented by Arthur's court, and in particular by the greatest warrior of the court, Lancelot, the lover of Queen Guinevere. But the very success of this romantic history produced an idealistic reaction. The Cistercian prose *Queste del Saint Graal* (c. 1215–30) celebrated the victory of spiritual over temporal power, and set up in place of Lancelot the less materially spectacular figures of Perceval, whose character is derived from the Great Fool of folk tradition, and Galahad, Lancelot's bastard son. It is they, and not Lancelot, who fully accomplish the eucharistic Grail Quest – a quest throughout which the Cistercian author elaborated a particularly vivid version of the retrospective typology to which I have already alluded. Galahad, for instance, is a type of Christ almost as Isaac was. The major difference is that one lived long before the birth of Christ, the other 454 years after. The typology is present even in his name. Galahad is a variant of Galaad, the Vulgate name of the district to the east of Jordan which in the Authorized Version is called Gilead. As a consequence of the allegorical interpretation of Jeremiah VIII, 22: 'Is there no balm in Gilead; is there no physician there? Why then is not the health of the daughter of my people recovered?' – the name had come to be regarded as a verbal typology for Christ. Nor is it in name only that Galahad typologizes Christ, as may be seen even from a brief passage which occurs in the simplified translation which Sir Thomas Malory (c. 1408–71) called *The Noble Tale of the Sankegreall:*

> The Castell of Maydyns betokenyth the good soulys that were in preson before the Incarnacion of oure Lorde Jesu Cryste. And the seven knyghtes betokenyth the seven dedly synes that regned that tyme in the worlde. And I may lyckyn the good knyght Galahad unto the Sonne of the Hyghe Fadir that lyght within a maydyn and bought all the soules oute of thralle: so ded sir Galahad delyver all the may-dyns oute of the woofull castell.

> (Vinaver, p. 651)

Arthur's prophecy at the beginning of the Grail quest is well known:

D

'Alas!' seyde kynge Arthure unto sir Gawayne, 'ye have nygh slayne me for the avow that ye have made, for thorow you ye have berauffte me the fayryst and the trewyst of knyghthode that ever was sene togydir in ony realme of the worlde. For whan they departe frome hense I am sure they all shall never mete more togydir in thys worlde, for they shall dye many in the queste. And so hit forthynkith nat me a litill, for I have loved them as well as my lyff'

(Vinaver, p. 635)

The appearance of the Grail at Arthur's court corresponds in fact to the stone cut without hands which in Nebuchadnezzar's dream overthrew the statue which represented the *translatio imperii*.

The subject of this chapter is the medieval allegorization of time and history. In Chapter 2 I indicated by way of an analysis of *Revelation* that alphabetical and numerical allegory provided especially powerful images for the directed course of time. The tradition continued into the medieval and later periods. Thus, at some time before 597, when St Columba of Iona composed his Latin cosmogonic and eschatological hymn, the *Altus Prosator*, he chose a form which corresponded closely to the content – an account of the beginning and end of the world. It may be significant that on the authority of some good MSS., the poem should be regarded as 360 lines long (the year according to Genesis had a length of 360 days), and that it consists of 23 stanzas with a refrain; a total, in other words, of 24 stanzas, corresponding to the hours of the day. It is certainly significant that the stanzas are arranged acrostically, the first beginning with A (*Altus Prosator*), the second with B (*Bonos creavit angelos*), and so on to Z (*Zelus ignis furibundos*). Because J and I, V, U and W are identical, J, U and W are omitted. The meaning is again to be found in Christ's phrase, 'I am Alpha and Omega, the first and the last' (Revelation, I 11). The poem deals with the first and last things of history, a history which may also figuratively be regarded as a completed day or a completed year.

The tradition continued through the Middle Ages into the Renaissance, and is particularly well exemplified in the poetry of Edmund Spenser (1552–99). I end this chapter with a quotation from Alastair Fowler's fine study of numerology and iconography in the *Faerie Queene*, a quotation in which he describes Kent Hieatt's pioneer study of *Epithalamion:*

> Every student of Spenser is now indebted to Professor Kent Hieatt for his brilliant discovery of the number symbolism by which *Epithalamion* is metrically and structurally ordered. He has shown us . . . that the twenty-four stanzas and 365 long lines of the poem represent the measure of the day in hours and of the year in days; while further line-totals imitate the apparent daily movement of the sun relative to the fixed stars. Even the proper disproportion between the hours of daylight and darkness at the summer solstice (when the action of *Epithalamion* takes place) is indicated by a change in the refrain at a numerically significant point. Nor does this numerology merely constitute an external husk, a static frame within which the real poem proceeds. As Hieatt demonstrates, the sequence of the poem's images, even the meaning of many of its lines, cannot be fully understood except in terms of the structure of number symbolism. The analogy between the repetition of the seasons and the perpetuation of life through human generation is a part of the content; so that the numerology which imitates the year's cycle makes a dynamic contribution to the unfolding of the meaning.
>
> (*Spenser and the Numbers of Time*, p. 3)

4
Medieval Theories of Allegory

When the Roman emperor, Julian the Apostate (332–63 A.D.) came to the throne in 361, one of the first acts in his campaign against Christianity – by then the official religion of the Empire – was to forbid Christian children the old 'Greek' education. The importance attached to this measure shows how far Christians had already adapted classical educational theories and practices to their own purposes. Christian ideas and ideals had not originally been expressed in the categories of Greek and Roman scholarship and philosophy, but to gain attention from the educated classes of the Empire, it had proved necessary for them to be translated into terms which an educated Greek or Roman found easier to accept. The process is already visible in some of the Gospels and Pauline epistles; by the time of Julian, it was far advanced. Julian's measures, even within his own short reign, proved abortive. The curriculum of the medieval grammar school or university has an unbroken connection with that of the schools which during the Roman Empire had adapted themselves to make use of biblical and patristic, as well as classical, material.

In the Christian grammar school, the process of adaptation was particularly important. The great Latin poets, especially Virgil, Ovid and Statius, remained the most important curriculum authors. Yet it was impossible to understand their poetry without some considerable knowledge of the pagan mythology which the Church regarded as standing totally in opposition to itself. The quarrel between poetry and Christianity in the Middle Ages often resembled the earlier struggle of poetry with philosophy in the time of Plato. In both cases, one possible solution was the concept of myth as allegory. Pagan and Christian mythographers elaborated this concept, and their work, which extends in an unbroken chain from the later Empire to the seventeenth century, culminated in the encyclopedic *De Genealogia Deorum Gentilium*, 'Concerning the Genealogy of the Pagan Gods', which Giovanni Boccaccio (1313–75) compiled towards the end of his life. Ostensibly the book was a conspectus of classical mythology, but virtually every divinity and demigod whose name is mentioned received some kind of allegorical interpretation. Boccaccio in fact wrote his encyclopedia as a defence of classical studies, and in particular of classical poetry, which he saw as primarily narrative, and primarily concerned with the events and personages of classical mythology. From his point of view, all worthwhile narrative was fable (*fabula*); it contained, that is to say, a kernel of vital meaning concealed beneath a shell of fictitious and often improbable narrative. The shell of classical poetry consisted of myths about the gods; the kernel was the allegorical meaning which underlay the shell. Classical poetry was Boccaccio's primary concern, but the method of interpretation which he applied might be, and frequently was, used by vernacular poets for their own compositions. The book was widely read in Western Europe, and affected the visual arts, as well as poetry and prose. I quote his definition of fable, and his further subdivision into four classes. (The fourth was probably intended to cover popular narratives which it was difficult to fit into an allegorical scheme.)

A fable is a connected utterance which, under the appearance of fiction, is exemplary or demonstrative, and which reveals its author's purpose only when the shell of fiction has been removed. And thus, if something savoury is discovered under the veil of fable, the composition of fables will not be a completely useless activity. I believe that fables form a four-fold species; and the first of those – i.e. when we represent brute beasts or even inanimate objects, as talking among themselves – altogether lacks, it seems to me, literal truth. In this category, the most important author was Aesop, a Greek to be respected not merely because he belonged to classical antiquity, but also for his serious moral purpose. And even granted that, for the most part, it is the urban and rural vulgar who make use of him, one must remember that Aristotle, a man of superhuman ability and prince of the Peripatetic philosophers, from time to time did not hesitate to refer to him in his books.

The second species not infrequently gives the superficial appearance of mingling the fabulous with truth, as, for instance, if we describe how the daughters of Minyas, spinning and despising the orgies of Bacchus, were turned into bats, and how the comrades of the sailor Acestis, as a result of their plot to kidnap Bacchus, were turned into fish. From the beginning the most ancient poets, whose task it was to cloak with fictions divine and human affairs alike, have invented such legends. The more sublime among subsequent poets have followed them, and exalted the species, while at the same time one must allow that a few comic poets have degraded it because they cared more for the applause of the senseless vulgar than for their own reputation.

The third species resembles historical fact rather than fable. Famous poets have used this in many different ways. Writers of epic, no matter to what degree they may appear to write factually, as Virgil, when he describes Aeneas tossed by the storm at sea, and Homer with Ulysses tethered to the mast of the ship, for fear he should succumb to the song of the Sirens, still realize that something far different from their apparent subject is concealed beneath the veil. So also the more reputable comic poets, like Plautus and Terence, have made use of this species in their dialogue, understanding nothing more than the literal meaning of the words, but wishing nevertheless to describe by their art the manners and words of different kinds of men, and at the same time to teach and warn their readers. And as fables of this kind deal with universals, even if the narrative has no actual basis in historical fact, it is still probable, or at least possible. Our accusers have no cause to reject this mode, since our Lord Christ so often made use of it in his parables.

The fourth species possesses absolutely no surface or hidden truth, since it is the invention of silly old women.

(XIV, ix)

As a trope, an incidental rhetorical device or ornament, allegory had already in Roman times been subjected to categorization. A brief analysis, for instance, is to be found in *Institutio Oratoria* VIII, vi, 44–59 of the Roman writer Quintilian (c. A.D. 37–100) whose work I have already quoted. Quintilian understands the word in a very broad sense, derived from the etymology. Allegory, he observes, presents either (1) one thing in words and another in meaning or else (2) something absolutely opposed to the meaning of the words (*aut aliud verbis aliud sensu ostendit aut etiam interim contrarium*). Under (1) he discusses the use of metaphor, simile and riddle (*aenigma*) in a way which bears a direct relation to the modern use of the term 'allegory'. Under (2) he discusses figures in which the effect is produced by an element of irony, whether it took the form of sarcasm, *asteismos*, contradiction or proverbs. I shall return later to *asteismos*, but in general it may be said that ironic figures would not nowadays be regarded as forming part of allegory. Quintilian's complete doctrine, however, became part of the schoolmaster's stock in trade. It is found almost unchanged in *Etymologiae* I, xxxvii, 22–30, part of the section on rhetoric in the encyclopedic work by Isidore of Sevile (c. A.D. 560–636), which so much influenced the Middle Ages.

Biblical allegory was first categorized in terms of differing levels of figurative meaning. John Cassian (c. A.D. 360–435) was apparently the first Latin writer to formulate the familiar four levels – the literal: the allegorical strictly so called, applying the passage to Christ and the Church Militant: the tropological or moral, understanding it of the soul and its virtues: and the anagogical, applying it to the heavenly realities and the Church Triumphant (*Collationes*, xiv, 8). In a rough way, this parallels the system, quoted at the end of the first chapter, which Sallustius proposed for the interpretation of classical myth. Bede (c. A.D. 673–735) appears to have been the first to assimilate biblical allegory completely to the categories of the classical grammarians and rhetoricians. His *De*

Schematibus et Tropis Sacrae Scripturae, 'Concerning the Figures and Tropes of Holy Scripture', written between 691 and 703, demonstrates that the ornaments of classical rhetoric were also to be found in the Old and New Testaments. 'De Allegoria', section 12 of the second chapter of the brief treatise, follows the pattern established by Quintilian and Isidore, and discusses allegory in terms of irony, *antiphrasis, aenigma, charientismos, paroemia* and sarcasm. Those sections we may safely ignore. The last, and from our point of view the most important, sub-section is headed 'De Asteismo'.

In classical literary theory, *asteismos*, derived from Greek ἄστυ, 'town' (often with particular reference to Athens), meant 'wit of an urbane, refined sort', usually depending on a play of differing or opposed meanings within a word or phrase. The wit of biblical allegory Bede would certainly have attributed to God, the Creator. He would have agreed with the fifteenth century Scottish poet, Robert Henryson (as with the author of *Beowulf* and the seventeenth century metaphysical poets) that 'God in all his werkis wittie is'.

Bede discussed the term thus. (In translating, I have been forced to introduce several emendations. The text printed by Giles contains several corrupt readings.)

Asteismos is a trope that has many levels and many applications. It is defined as any saying which lacks rustic directness, and has been sufficiently refined with urbane wit, as for instance, 'I would they were even cut off which trouble you. One should certainly notice that allegory is sometimes factual, sometimes verbal only. It is factual, for instance, in the scriptural text that Abraham had two sons, the one by a bondmaid and the other by a freewoman, as the Apostle expounds it. It is verbal only, as in Isaiah XI, 'There will come forth a rod out of the stem of Jesse, and a flower will grow out of its root'. By this is signified that our Lord and Saviour would be born from the line of David by the virgin Mary. Sometimes one and the same thing is allegorically signified factually and verbally; factually, as in Genesis

XXXVII, 'They have sold Joseph to the Ishmaelites for thirty pieces of silver': verbally, as in Zechariah XI, 'They weighed for my price thirty pieces of silver'. Again, factually, as in 1 Kings XVI (i.e., 1 Samuel XVI), 'Now David was ruddy, and fair of aspect, and Samuel anointed him in the midst of his brothers'; verbally, as in Solomon's Song V, My beloved is white and ruddy, the chiefest among thousands'. Both of those mystically signify the Mediator between God and men, adorned with wisdom and virtue, but that He was made red by the effusion of his own blood, and that He was anointed by God the father with the oil of gladness in front of his brothers.

Again, verbal or factual allegory figuratively conveys a meaning which in some passages is historical, in others typological, in others tropological (that is, concerned with the conduct of life), in others anagogical (that is, a meaning which leads us upwards to heaven). History serves as a figure for history when the work of the first six or seven days is compared to the same number of ages of this world. Words serve as a figure for history when the saying of the patriarch Jacob in Genesis XLIX – 'Judah is a lion's whelp; from the prey, my son, thou art gone up' etc. – is interpreted in terms of the reign and victories of David. Words serve spiritually as a figure for Christ or the Church when the same saying of the patriarch is faithfully accepted as referring to the Passion and Resurrection of our Lord. Again, a factual allegory designates a tropological, that is a moral, perfection, as in Genesis XXXVII: the coat of many colours which the patriarch Jacob made for his son Joseph is also an indirect representation of the grace of diverse virtues with which God the father has ordained and gives us always to be clad until the end of our life. Verbal allegory signifies the same moral perfection, as in 'Let your loins be girt and your lamps burning' etc. Factual allegory expresses an anagogical meaning, that is, one leading to the things above, as in 'Enoch, the seventh generation from Adam, was taken bodily from this world.' This is a figurative prophecy of the Sabbath of future blessedness which, after the good works of this world performed in six ages, is reserved for the elect at the end. Verbal allegory points out the same joys of the heavenly life, as in Matthew XXIV, 'For wheresoever the carcass is, there will the eagles be gathered together' – because where the Mediator between God and men is in body, there certainly even at this instant the souls of the just have been raised to heaven, and when the glory of the Resurrection has been celebrated, their bodies also will be gathered to the same place.

Frequently in one and the same fact or word, the historical sense, together with the mystical concerning Christ or the Church, and tropology and anagogy, are figuratively expressed. Take, for instance, the phrase, 'the Temple of the Lord'. In terms of history, it is the house which Solomon built: in terms of allegory, it is the body of the Lord, about which John speaks in his second chapter, 'Destroy this temple, and in three days I will raise it up.' Or it is his Church, to whom is said, 'The temple of God is holy, which temple ye are.' By tropology it is each of the faithful, to whom is said in 1 Corinthian III, 'Know ye not that your bodies are the temple of the Holy Spirit, which is in you?' By anagogy, it is the mansions of joy above, to which aspired the man who said, 'Blessed are they who dwell in thy house, O Lord; they will praise thee for ever and ever.' In the same way, with respect to what is said in Psalm CXLVII, 'Praise the Lord, O Jerusalem; praise thy God, O Zion. For he hath strengthened the bars of thy gates; he hath blessed thy children within thee' – it is correct and possible for this to be accepted as referring to the citizens of Jerusalem on earth, the Church of Christ, the elect soul also, and the heavenly fatherland – according, that is, to history, to allegory, to tropology, and to anagogy. We use the word allegory in reference to the Church, following the example of the most learned writer Gregory, who in his *Moralia* was accustomed to limit the proper use of the word allegory to facts or expressions which were interpretable in terms of Christ or the Church.

Bede's distinction between verbal and factual allegory is important. Verbal allegory is a trope: it is a use of figurative language to convey prophetic information. Factual allegory is New Testament typology. God, as author of the universe wittily arranges that his creation shall operate at two levels, the immediate and the prophetic. Isaac was Isaac, but he was also a prophecy of Christ. It should also be noted that Bede uses the term allegory to cover all four levels of scriptural interpretation, historical, typological, tropological and anagogical. One might expect the historical to be identical with the literal but Bede justifies his distinction by such examples as the parallel between the six days of creation and the six ages of the world, or Jacob's prophecy interpreted as referring to David rather than Christ. For him, in other words, the historical is not necessarily the same as the literal. Bede also indicates that the word allegory may be used in a more limited sense to cover only the second level of 'spiritual' meaning the typological – a usage which he defends by the authority of Gregory the Great (c. A.D. 540–604) in his influential *Expositio in Librum Iob sive Moralium Libri XXV*, 'Exposition of the Book of Job, or Twenty-Five Books of Moral Comment' – the *Moralia* as it is usually called. Both usages are to be found in the later Middle Ages, not infrequently in the same author. One may quote Thomas Aquinas (c. 1225–74) in his *Summa Theologica* I, 10, a passage which also has considerable relevance for Bede's distinction between verbal and factual allegory:

The author of Holy Scripture is God, in whose power it is to signify his meaning, not by words only (as man also can do), but also by things themselves. So, whereas in every other science things are signified by words, this science [of sacred doctrine] has the property that the things signified by the words have themselves also a signification. Therefore that first signification whereby words signify things belongs to the first sense, the historical or literal. That signification whereby things signified by words have themselves also a signification is called the spiritual sense, which is based on the literal and presupposes it. Now this spiritual sense has a threefold division. For as the Apostle says, the Old Law is a figure of the New Law, and Dionysius says the *New Law itself is a figure of future glory*. Again, in the New Law, whatever our Head has done is a type of what we ought to do. Therefore, so far as the things of the Old Law signify the things of the New Law, there is the allegorical sense; so far as the things done in Christ, or so far as the things which signify Christ, are signs of what we ought to do, there is the moral sense. But so far as they signify what relates to eternal glory, there is the anagogical sense.

A few lines later, Aquinas adds, 'Allegory (i.e. the term) alone stands for the three spiritual senses.'

Of the writers so far quoted in this chapter, Boccaccio certainly had vernacular literature at least in the back of his mind, while neither Bede nor Aquinas would have denied that biblical allegory might be used in vernacular composition. Dante Alighieri (1265–1321), however, is the first to relate a theory of allegory, closely resembling that advanced by Aquinas, directly to the study of at least some kinds of vernacular literature. His *Convivio* (c. 1306) is a banquet of knowledge set out by the poet for the benefit of those who are prevented from finding a seat at the table of the blest. The blest are those who have been able to satisfy man's natural desire for knowledge. The poet does not regard himself as one of their number, but like the Syro-Phoenician woman in Mark VII, 27–8, he has gathered crumbs from the table, and thus gained material for his own banquet. 'The meats of this banquet will be arranged in fourteen courses, that is, fourteen *canzoni* (odes), whereof both love and virtue are the subject-matter' (*Tractate* I, i.). The meat however will be accompanied by bread, the prose tractates in which Dante sets out the literal and allegorical meanings of the poems. If the scheme had been completed, Dante intended it to form a compendium of universal knowledge.

Dante's first *canzone* appears at the beginning of the second tractate of the *Convivio*, and is at once followed by a statement of the theory of allegory in vernacular composition:

It is meet for this exposition to be both literal and allegorical. And to make this intelligible, it should be known that writings can be understood and ought to be expounded chiefly in four senses. The first is called literal, and this is that sense which does not go beyond the strict limits of the letter; the second is called allegorical and this is disguised under the cloak of such stories, and is a truth hidden under a beautiful fiction (*ed è una veritude ascosa sotto bella menzogna* – literally 'a beautiful lie'. The Platonic Idea of Beauty is as important as the lack of

literal truth, and Dante is the first allegorical theorist to emphasize it.)
Thus Ovid says that Orpheus with his lyre made beasts tame, and
trees and stones move towards himself; that is to say that the wise man
by the instrument of his voice makes cruel hearts grow mild and
humble, and those who have not the life of Science and of Art move
to his will, while they who have no rational life are as it were like
stones. And wherefore this disguise was invented by the wise will be
shown in the last Tractate but one. Theologians indeed do not appre-
hend this sense in the same fashion as poets; but, inasmuch as my
intention is to follow here the custom of poets, I will take the allegorical sense after the manner which poets use.

The third sense is called moral; and this sense is that for which
teachers ought as they go through writings intently to watch for their
own profit and that of their hearers; as in the Gospel when Christ
ascended the Mount to be transfigured, we may be watchful of his
taking with Himself the three Apostles out of the twelve; whereby
morally it may be understood that for the most secret affairs we ought
to have few companions.

The fourth sense is called anagogic, that is, above the senses; and
this occurs when a writing is spiritually expounded, which even in the
literal sense by the things signified likewise gives intimation of higher
matters belonging to the eternal glory; as can be seen in that song of
the prophet which says that, when the people of Israel went up out of
Egypt, Judea was made holy and free. And although it be plain that
this is true according to the letter, that which is spiritually understood
is not less true, namely, that when the soul issues forth from sin she
is made holy and free as mistress of herself.

(II, i.)

In the context of the earlier parts of this chapter, it should be
obvious that Dante uses the word allegory in the more specialized
of the two possible senses. The allegory of the theologians, with
which he contrasts that of the poets, is typology – special allegory,
as it might be called, in distinction from general allegory, which
includes tropology and anagogy together with typology. For
typology Dante substitutes something which approximates to the
allegorical exposition of classical myth as discussed by Sallustius

or Boccaccio. His treatment of Orpheus is at the level which Sallustius would have called psychic, and Sallustius, the reader will remember, regarded physical and psychic myths as particularly suitable for poetry. Dante gives a psychic interpretation of the Lady of the first *can\zone* when he calls her 'the fairest and most honourable Daughter of the Emperor of the Universe, on whom Pythagoras conferred the name of philosophy' (II, xvi).

The exclusion of typology nevertheless remains somewhat surprising, more especially when Dante found no difficulty in exemplifying the tropological and anagogical level with biblical references (Mark IX, 2–8: Psalm CXIV). But I confess some inclination to minimize the difficulty. In poetry, after all, mythological allegory is considerably more frequent than typological, and Dante may have felt, at least when he wrote the *Convivio*, that classical myth met his requirements of 'truth hidden under a beautiful fiction' more accurately than any Old Testament incident. It is certainly true that for the elucidation of the *can\zoni*, which form the meat of the *Convivio*, typological allegory was unnecessary, while mythological was essential. Dante therefore had immediate grounds for including one, but excluding the other.

Dante may have left the *Convivio* incomplete because his energies were increasingly devoted to the *Divina Commedia*. In this he did not abandon mythological allegory, as may for instance be seen in the treatment of the giants, Ephialtes and Antaeus, who appear in *Inferno* XXXI. In religious poetry, however, which attempted a universal theme, the introduction of typology was inevitable, and Dante made allowance for it in the Latin letter which he wrote to Can Grande della Scala on the interpretation of the *Divina Commedia*, and which repeats, with significant variations, the doctrine and one of the examples quoted in the *Conviviorom*

The meaning of this work is not of one kind only; rather the work may be described as 'polysemous', that is, having several meanings; for the first meaning is that which is conveyed by the letter, and the next is that which is conveyed by what the letter signifies; the former of which is called literal, while the latter is called allegorical, or mystical. And for the better illustration of this method of exposition we may apply it to the following verses: 'When Israel went out of Egypt, the house of Jacob from a people of strange language; Judah was his sanctuary, and Israel his dominion.' For if we consider the letter alone, the thing signified to us is the going out of the Children of Israel from Egypt in the time of Moses; if the allegory, our redemption through Christ is signified; if the moral sense, the conversion of the soul from the sorrow and misery of sin to a state of grace is signified; if the anagogical, the passing of the sanctified soul from the bondage of the corruption of this world to the liberty of everlasting glory is signified. And although these mystical meanings are called by various names, they may one and all in a general sense be termed allegorical, inasmuch as they are different from the literal and historical; for the word 'allegory' is so called from the Greek *alleon*, which in Latin is *alienum* or *diversum*.

This being understood, it is clear that the subject, with regard to which the alternative meanings are brought into play, must be twofold. And therefore the subject of this work must be considered in the first place from the point of view of the literal meaning, and next from that of the allegorical interpretation. The subject, then, of the whole work, taken in the literal sense only, is the state of souls after death, pure and simple. For on and about that the argument of the whole work turns. If, however, the work be regarded from the allegorical point of view, the subject is man according as by his merits or demerits in the exercise of his free will he is deserving of reward or punishment by justice.

(7–8)

In *Purgatorio* II, the description of the arrival of the ship of redeemed souls at the foot of Mount Purgatory, Dante made direct allegorical use of the biblical text which he quoted to Can Grande (Psalm CXIV, 1):

> Poi come più e più verso noi venne
>   l'uccel divino, più chiaro appariva;
>   per che l'occhio da presso nol sostenne,

> ma chinail giuso; e quei sen venne a riva
> con un vasello snelletto e leggiero,
> tanto che l' acqua nulla ne inghiottiva.
>
> Da poppa stava il celestial nocchiero,
> tal che parea beato per iscritto;
> e più di cento spirti entro sediero
>
> '*In exitu Israel de Egitto*,'
> cantavan tutti insieme ad una voce,
> con quanto di quel salmo è poscia scritto.

(37–48)

(Then as more and more towards us came the bird divine [the angel pilot of the ship], brighter yet he appeared, wherefore mine eye endured him not near: but I bent it down, and he came on to the shore with a vessel so swift and light that the waters nowise drew it in. On the stern stood the celestial pilot, such, that blessedness seemed writ upon him, and more than a hundred spirits sat within. '*In exitu Israel de Aegypto*' sang they all together with one voice, with what of that psalm is thereafter written.)

The redeemed souls after death compare themselves to the Israelites after their departure from Egypt; typologically, they celebrate their redemption through Christ; tropologically, their conversion from the sorrow and misery of sin to the state of grace; anagogically, their passage as sanctified souls from the bondage of the corruption of this world to the liberty of everlasting glory. Appropriately, the assumed time within the narrative, is dawn on Easter Day.

5
Allegory and the Individual

Myth and ritual in mystery religions, the philosophic allegory of
Plato or Apuleius, the tropological level of scriptural interpretation – all those have one thing in common. This primary relevance
is for the individual, whether as initiate, student or Christian. The
proper conduct of life and the final destination of the soul may
depend on a full understanding of text or ritual. It is not then surprising that in the Middle Ages when allegorical ways of writing
came to dominate, the emphasis tended to move from the external
to the internal world, a development evident in the very title of the
relatively brief but enormously influential epic of the Christian
Latin poet Prudentius (c. A.D. 348–410), the *Psychomachia*. The
title (Gk. ψυχομαχία) originally meant something like 'desperate
fighting, a fight to the finish', but Prudentius clearly intended it to
mean 'the battle in, and for, the soul'.

He introduced his poem by way of a tropological and typological analysis of the Old Testament story of Abraham. For him, as
still, in the late fourteenth century, for William Langland, Abraham represented Faith, the first of the three theological virtues:

> And thanne mette I with a man a Mydlenten Sondaye
> As hore as an hawethorne, and Abraham he highte
> I frayned hym first fram whennes he come,
> And of whennes he were and whider that he thoughte.
> 'I am Feith', quod that freke, 'it falleth noughte to lye,
> And of Abrahames hous an heraud of armes.'
>
> (*Piers Plowman*, B XVI, 172–7)

Abraham represents Faith because, even when he found himself at
the age of ninety-nine a childless man, and later still when he accepted

E

God's command to sacrifice the son of his extreme old age, he continued to accept the promise, 'I will make of thee a great nation' (Genesis XII, 2). He was not himself a type of Christ, but by the exercise of faith recognized that he had encountered types of Christ and the Trinity – Melchizedek, king and priest of Salem (Gensis XIV, 18–20), the three men who visited him in the plains of Mamre (XVIII, 1–33), and in particular his own son Isaac. Prudentius mentions all those incidents, but reserves his greatest emphasis for another which preceded them, Abraham's rescue of his nephew Lot, who had chosen to live in the Cities of the Plain, and who had been made prisoner by the invading forces of the kings Amraphel, Arioch, Chedorlaomer and Tidal (Genesis XIV).

There is a certain parallel between Prudentius's treatment of this story and Henryson's handling of the myth of Orpheus and Eurydice, to which I referred in Chapter 1. Lot, like Eurydice, represents the fallen lower powers of the human soul; Abraham, like Orpheus, the higher, which, strengthened by faith, are able to redeem the lower. For Prudentius, in other words, the kings who capture Lot represent the powers of sin in the soul, powers which Abraham must defeat before he is capable or worthy of meeting Melchizedek and the three men, or of begetting Isaac. Tropologically, the battle is the crucial event in the history of Abraham, and correspondingly the main body of Prudentius's poem is a general account of the struggle between personified virtues and vices for the possession of the soul:

> non simplex natura hominis; nam viscera limo
> effigiata premunt animum, contra ille sereno
> editus adflatu nigrantis carcere cordis
> aestuat et sordes arta inter vincla recusat.
> spiritibus pugnant variis lux atque tenebrae
> distantesque animat duplex substantia vires,
> donec praesidio Christus deus adsit et omnes
> virtutum gemmas conponat sede piata.

(904–11)

The nature of man is divided; for the entrails, fashioned from slime, oppress the soul, and in opposition the soul, child of the calm breath of God, rages in the prison of the black heart and, amid her constricting chains, refuses filth. Light and darkness, accompanied by their mutually hostile spirits, contend, and the divided essence of man gives life to opposite powers, until Christ the Lord comes to take command, and arranges all the jewels of the virtues in settings which have been made pure.

The opposition of personified abstractions – *Fides*, for instance, and *Veterum Cultura Deorum*, *Pudicitia* and *Sodomita Libido* – gives rise to the main action of the poem, but as the *Praefatio* establishes, Prudentius had it equally in his power to develop an abstract theme in terms of historical figures and events – in the present instance, Abraham, Lot and the others. The abstract plot receives body, as it were, from the parallel historical and tropological narrative, which in turn it clarifies and illuminates. In the body of the poem, Prudentius sometimes achieves similar incidental juxtapositions, as for instance when he describes Pudicitia wiping her sword after the death of Libido:

> *dixerat haec et laeta Libidinis interfectae*
> *morte Pudicitia gladium Jordanis in undis*
> *abluit infectum*

(98–100)

(When she had said this, rejoicing at the death of lust whom she had slain, Chastity cleansed her tainted sword in the waves of Jordan.)

The reference to the baptism of Christ gives an almost startling effect of reality and significance. Indeed, one of the great virtues of the form which Prudentius developed was this power to move rapidly from one level of reference to another – from abstract to historical or tropological, even typological and anagogical. The dominating level might be either the abstract or the tropological/

historical. *Piers Plowman*, like the *Psychomachia*, keeps for the most part to the level of abstraction; in general, the main characters have such names as Mede, Wit, Reason. Faith, Hope and Charity, however, appear as Abraham, Moses and the Good Samaritan who is also Christ. The allegorical figures who appear in Dante's *Divina Commedia* almost all have a historical identity. Cato, who represents the four cardinal virtues, Prudence, Temperance, Fortitude and Justice, may serve as an example. In Arthurian romance, most of the figures are entirely fictitious, but they are imagined as historical personages in a more or less historical setting, and are given an allegorical meaning.

The most generally familiar account of Prudentius's poem is to be found in C. S. Lewis's *The Allegory of Love*. Lewis avoids any reference to the *Praefatio*, and in general, I would say, underestimates or distorts the poetic value of the *Psychomachia*. One must however agree with his observation that as narrative the poem has a serious flaw. In an Aristotelian sense, it lacks action; the plot is nothing more than a series of semi-static, occasionally slightly ludicrous, encounters. Prudentius should have given more study to the narrative art with which in Genesis the saga of Abraham is developed.

The history of psychological allegory after Prudentius's day is largely that of the development of extended narrative. A battle, or more frequently a series of individual encounters, remains almost invariably at the heart of the action. For narrative effectiveness, the battle came to form the climax of a plot, or interwoven plots, which involved something more than mere fighting. The action came to turn not so much on the battle as on the objective for which the battle was fought. That objective inevitably was salvation, and, almost equally inevitably, the dominant narrative device came to be the pilgrimage or quest – the Pilgrim's Progress from this world to that which is to come, as John Bunyan still put it in the latter part of the seventeenth century. Where common humanity received the greater allegorical emphasis, as in the *Pilgrimage of the Life of Man*, translated by John Lydgate (c. 1370–1450) from the French of Guillaume de Deguileville (c. 1294–1360), in *Piers Plowman*, or the work of Bunyan, the metaphor of the pilgrimage dominated. When the allegory was aimed at a more restricted courtly audience, the emphasis fell on the knightly quest, as exemplified by the Grail romances, *Sir Gawain and the Green Knight* (c. 1375–1400), Tasso's *Gierusalemme Liberata* (1574), or Spenser's *Faerie Queene* (1590, 1596, 1609).

Quest and pilgrimage were the dominant narrative devices, but in Chapter 1 I referred to another, the otherworld journey, which became almost equally important. The theme was developed as an allegory of abstractions by Bernardus Sylvestris (*floruit* c. 1150) in *De Mundi Universitate* and by Alan of Lille (c. 1128–1203) in his Latin epic, *Anticlaudianus*, a work which Dante knew well, and which influenced him in the composition of his own otherworld journey, the *Divina Commedia*. Chaucer (c. 1343–1400) made a characteristic adaptation in his briefer narratives, the *House of Fame* and the *Parlement of Fowles*. James I of Scotland (1394–1437) made use of it in his *Kingis Quair*. I have more than once mentioned the otherworld journey in Henryson's *Orpheus and Eurydice*, with which one should compare the planetary parliament in *The Testament of Cresseid*. Spenser, like Ariosto, Tasso and Milton, includes more than one otherworld journey in his major poem. During the twentieth century the theme returned to popularity. Much of the best science fiction written in the past fifty years or so has developed the allegoric and satiric potential of the otherworld journey.

The *Summarium*, which in some MSS. is attached to the *Anticlaudianus*, contains a scholastic analysis of the poem, of particular importance for the Chaucerian and Spenserian developments of the form. I translate the opening sentences:

Because the four Makers (*artifices*), God, Nature, Fortune and Sin, form the subject of this work, the poem deals with the operations of each. Those of the first Maker, that is, of God, are fourfold: in mind, in matter, in form and in government. Those of Nature are twofold: one regarded in terms of her original nature, free from all corruption, as the operation of Nature was before the fall of Adam; the other as things now are, after the fall of Adam, when Nature has been tainted by a host of corruptions. Those of Fortune are also twofold: one in terms of prosperity, and one of adversity. Sin has one operation only, to deprave. As a consequence, the book of which this forms the subject matter contains nine divisions [i.e., the nine books of the complete poem. The number is significant. Cf. the nine orders of angels, the nine spheres, the nine circles of Dante's Hell, etc.]. In the first part, consisting of the first four books, the subject matter is equally the operations of Nature and of God, because through the operations of Nature, the invisible works of God are revealed. The second part, Books V and VI, is concerned with the operation of God. The third part, Book VII and the beginning of Book VIII, is concerned with the operation of Fortune. The fourth part, the end of Book VIII and Book IX, is concerned with the operation of Sin.

(Bossuat, p. 199)

The fourth part of the poem is in fact a *psychomachia*.

Since 1936, when C. S. Lewis published *The Allegory of Love*, the English-speaking world has been most familiar with that form of psychological allegory best represented by the first part of the *Roman de la Rose*, which its author, Guillaume de Lorris, left incomplete at some time in the first half of the thirteenth century, and which centres on the relationship between courtly lovers. Lewis's book sets out the details of the emergence of this form and its subsequent developments. Guillaume unfortunately left no analysis of his own literary aims and procedures. Lewis's account however is well known and widely accepted:

> Guillaume de Lorris differs from his modern successor in some important respects. In the first place, he practically abolishes the hero, as one of his dramatis personae, by reducing him to the colourless teller of

the tale. The whole poem is in the first person and we look through the lover's eyes, not at him. In the second place he removes the heroine entirely. Her character is distributed among personifications. This seems, at first a startling device, but Guillaume knows what he is about. You cannot really have the lady, and, say, the lady's Pride, walking about on the same stage as if they were entities on the same plane. Nor is it unnatural for a lover to regard his courtship as an adventure, not with a single person, but with that person's varying moods, some of which are his friends and some his enemies. A man need not go to the Middle Ages to discover that his mistress is many women as well as one, and that sometimes the woman he hoped to meet is replaced by a very different woman. Accordingly, the lover in the Romance is concerned not with a single 'lady', but with a number of 'moods' or 'aspects' of that lady who alternately help and hinder his attempts to win her love, symbolized by the Rose.

(p. 118)

One should perhaps add that Lewis has here at least partly forgotten that the *Roman de la Rose* belongs to the family of the *Psychomachia*, and that Guillaume's position as ultimate narrator was rather less morally neutral than the casual reader might gather from his account.

The best known analysis by an English poet of his own psychological allegory is the *Letter* which Spenser addressed to Sir Walter Raleigh when in 1590 the first three books of the *Faerie Queene* were published. Spenser knew and accepted the allegorizations of Ariosto and the doctrine prefixed by Tasso to *Gierusalemme Liberata*. This last opens with the uncompromising statement, *L' Heroica Poesia, quasi animale, in cui due nature si congiungono, d'imitatione ed Allegoria è composta*, 'Heroic poetry, like an animal which is formed by the conjunction of two natures, is compounded from Imitation [i.e. Aristotelian mimesis] and Allegory.' Spenser's *Letter* notoriously contains its difficulties, but it remains not merely essential for any proper understanding of his own method and aims, but also relevant to the work of many

English poets in the centuries which followed. Milton, Dryden, Pope, Thomson, Wordsworth, Shelley and Keats (to name only the most important) were all influenced by the doctrine as well as the poetry of Spenser:

Sir knowing how doubtfully all Allegories may be construed, and this booke of mine, which I haue entituled the Faery Queene, being a continued Allegory, or darke conceit, I haue thought good aswell for auoyding of gealous opinions and misconstructions, as also for your better light in reading thereof, (being so by you commanded,) to discouer vnto you the general intention and meaning, which in the whole course thereof I haue fashioned, without expressing of any particular purposes or by-accidents therein occasioned. The generall end therefore of all the booke is to fashion a gentleman or noble person in vertuous and gentle discipline: Which for that I conceiued shoulde be most plausible and pleasing, being coloured with an historicall fiction, the which the most part of men delight to read, rather for variety of matter, then for profite of the ensample: I chose the historye of king Arthure, as most fitte for the excellency of his person, being made famous by many mens former workes, and also furthest from the daunger of enuy, and suspition of present time. In which I haue followed all the antique Poets historicall, first Homere, who in the Persons of Agamemnon and Vlysses hath ensampled a good gouernour and a vertuous man, the one in his Ilias, the other in his Odysseis: then Virgil, whose like intention was to doe in the person of Aeneas: after him Ariosto comprised them both in his Orlando: and lately Tasso disseuered them againe, and formed both parts in two persons, namely that part which they in Philosophy call Ethice, or vertues of a priuate man, coloured in his Rinaldo: The other named Politice in his Godfredo. By ensample of which excellente Poets, I labour to pourtraict in Arthure, before he was king, the image of a braue knight, perfected in the twelue priuate morall vertues, as Aristotle hath deuised, the which is the purpose of these first twelue bookes: which if I finde to be well accepted, I may be perhaps encoraged, to frame the other part of polliticke vertues in his person, after that hee came to be king. To some I know this Methode will seeme displeasaunt, which had rather haue good discipline deliuered plainly in way of precepts, or sermoned at large, as they vse, then thus clowdily enwrapped in Allegoricall deuises. But such, me seeme, should be satisfide with the vse of these dayes, seeing all things accounted by their showes, and nothing esteemed of, that is not delightfull and pleasing to commune sence. For this cause is Xenophon preferred before Plato, for that the one in the exquisite depth of his iudgement, formed a Commune welth such as it should be, but the other in the person of Cyrus and the Persians fashioned a gouernement such as might best be: So much more profitable and gratious is doctrine by ensample, then by rule. So haue I laboured to doe in the person of Arthure: whome I conceiue after his long education by Timon, to whom he was by Merlin deliuered to be brought up, so soon as he was borne of the Lady Igrayne, to haue seene in a dream or vision the Faery Queen, with whose excellent beauty rauished, he awaking resolued to seeke her out, and so being by Merlin armed, and by Timon throughly instructed, he went to seeke her forth in Faerye land. In that Faery Queene I meane glory in my generall intention, but in my particular I conceiue the most excellent and glorious person of our soueraine the Queene, and her kingdome in Faery land. And yet in some places els, I doe otherwise shadow her. For considering she beareth two persons, the one of a most royall Queene or Empresse, the other of a most vertuous and beautifull Lady, this latter part in some places I doe express in Belphoebe, fashioning her name according to your own excellent conceipt of Cynthia, (Phoebe and Cynthia being both names of Diana.) So in the person of Prince Arthure I sette forth magnificence in particular, which vertue for that (according to Aristotle and the rest) it is the perfection of all the rest, and conteineth in it them all, therefore in the whole course I mention the deedes of Arthure applyable to that vertue, which I write of in that booke. But of the xii. other vertues, I make xii. other knights the patrones, for the more variety of the history: Of which these three bookes contayn three, The first of the knight of the Redcrosse, in whome I express Holynes: The second of Sir Guyon, in whome I sette forth Temperaunce: The third of Britomartis a Lady Knight, in whom I picture Chastity.

6

Allegory and Satire

Psychological allegory of the kind we have been discussing deals with Everyman or Holiness or Mr Valiant-for-Truth: satire deals with Thomas Shadwell or Colley Cibber or William Fisher, elder in Mauchline parish, Ayrshire, Scotland. Allegory, in other words, is general, satire is particular – or so it might appear to the casual literary theorist. More often than not the actuality is different. Spenser's Holiness, for instance, is inextricably entangled with the Protestant Reformation and Mary Queen of Scots: Pope's Colley Cibber with cosmic dullness and anarchy; the name of Burns's Holy Willie has become a common, almost an abstract, noun. Nor is it difficult to resolve this apparent paradox. The generalities of allegory acquire power over the moral sense and the imagination by way of their relevance to the particular; the particularities of satire equally acquire more than passing relevance when they are seen in terms of a system of moral ideas which is generally accept-able. Very appropriately, John Butt (*The Augustan Age*, London, 1950, p. 71) adapted Wordsworth's description of a different type of poetry to fit Pope's satirical verse. 'Its object is truth, not individual and local, but general and operative; not stand-ing upon external testimony, but carried alive into the heart by passion; truth which is its own testimony.' From a different point of view, much the same might be said of the object of alle-gory.

Allegory and satire are in fact intimately connected. It is surpris-ing how often one gains a better understanding of an allegory by considering it as a satire, and *vice versa*.

Consider, for instance, the description of Vanity Fair in the

Pilgrim's Progress (a description which obviously and powerfully appealed to the satiric imagination of Thackeray):

> And, as in other fairs of less moment, there are the several rows and streets, under their proper names, where such and such wares are vended; so here likewise you have the proper places, rows, streets, (viz. countries and kingdoms,) where the wares of this fair are soonest to be found. Here is the *Britain Row*, the *French Row*, the *Italian Row*, the *Spanish Row*, the *German Row*, where several sorts of vanities are to be sold. But, as in other fairs, some one commodity is as the chief of all the fair, so the ware of *Rome* and her merchandise is greatly promoted in this fair; only our *English* nation, with some others, have taken a dislike thereat.

This surely is satire, not least in the packed implications of the final sentence. Equally clearly, I should say, the basic structure of Swift's satirical *Gulliver's Travels* is allegorical; the island of pigmies, the island of giants, the flying island, and the island of rational horses are all allegories of aspects of the human condition, which might perfectly well have found their way into an avowedly allegorical medieval or renaissance narrative. The form is that of the otherworld journey. In many of Blake's poems too allegory and satire are present together, but the distinction fades into imperceptibility:

> I wander thro' each charter'd street,
> Near where the charter'd Thames does flow
> And mark in every face I meet
> Marks of weakness, marks of woe.

London here is both the allegory of a state of mind and an actual city whose way of life totally offended Blake's religious principles.

Even from those few examples, the creative richness of the two modes in conjunction becomes obvious. Nor is this richness confined to incidents and incidentals. Successful literary allegory, whether it is found in the *Psychomachia*, the *Roman de la Rose*, the *Faerie Queene*, or the *Pilgrim's Progress*, usually depends on a more or less dramatic clash of opposites; the narrative shape may be complicated, as in the *Roman de la Rose* or the *Faerie Queene*, but it is necessarily there. The importance of thematic content to allegory goes without saying. If one combines the narrative form and thematic content of allegory with the detailed richness and stylized point of view found in good satire, one discovers literary forms of great potential. The *Pilgrim's Progress*, the *Life and Death of Mr Badman*, and *Gulliver's Travels*, for instance, mark important stages in the development of the English novel; the methods used by Bunyan and Swift are taken up by Fielding in the mock-heroic *Tom Jones*, and later by Jane Austen in the novels whose titles – *Pride and Prejudice, Sense and Sensibility, Persuasion* – almost recall the allegorical interludes of the sixteenth century. Very noticeably, the American novel, as exemplified by the work of Hawthorne and Melville, retained and developed this allegorical structure.

The development is not only English and American, but Western European. In particular, the origin of the satiric, realistic novel is to a great extent Spanish, and as A. A. Parker has shown in his *Literature and the Delinquent*, the Spanish picaresque novel takes its origins from the allegorical expression of the ideals of the Counter Reformation in Spain. These are expressed, he says, 'most explicitly in the religious literature, which in lyrical poems and morality plays presents from first to last countless allegories in which man enters into the world along what he thinks is the path of freedom, only to find that it is the road of enslavement to passion and the senses.'

Professor Parker, it will be noticed, links the emerging realistic novel directly to the allegorical morality play in the context of the Counter Reformation. (The cultural content in which the English novel later appeared is not entirely dissimilar – the commercial, industrial and scientific morality of the eighteenth century, and such reactions to it as the Methodism of the Wesleys.) In this chapter however I intend to show that an earlier crisis of belief and behaviour, the English and Scottish Renaissance and Reformation, brought allegory and satire creatively together in the morality play, which in turn, and partly as a consequence, developed into the poetic and realistic drama of Elizabethan and Jacobean England.

The morality belongs ultimately to the stock of the *Psychomachia*, and even in its earliest form it was necessarily something more than pure allegory. Realism of a kind helps to make the conflict of vice and virtue dramatically compelling, and in terms of the literary theories of the day such realism found appropriate expression in low style and a fairly wide range of comic incident. In the *Castle of Perseverance*, for instance, written before 1440, one extreme of comedy may be represented by the preliminary instruction, 'and he þat schal pley belyal loke þat he haue gunnepowdyr brennynge In pypys in hys handys and in hys erys and in hys ars whanne he gothe to batayl.' The other is the ironic, almost satiric fact that in Mankind's old age, after six of the seven deadly sins – Pride, Envy, Wrath, Gluttony, Lechery and Sloth – have been forcibly repelled from the castle battlements, he falls victim to the mere words of Avarice, and voluntarily abandons the castle.

Satire of this kind, however, remains entirely general. Humanum Genus, the hero of the *Castle of Perseverance*, is Mankind, Everyman, and no more; no-one has ever suggested a specific target for any part of the play. Yet to us with the advantage of hindsight, the inherent possibilities of the morality form for direct satiric comment are obvious – doubly obvious in view of the popular appeal of morality performances, and the religious authority which they at least appeared to possess. The morality was in fact open to exploitation in a multitude of ways: it was a weapon for anyone who felt able to identify himself or his own cause with the side of God and the virtues, that of his enemies with the world, the flesh and the devil. Nor was it limited to Christian values; the form

might be adapted to any ethical scheme which involved the possibility of conflict, and to secular as well as to spiritual affairs.

The first extant play in the British Isles to adapt the morality
form to secular politics is *Magnyfycence* (1515–16), written by
John Skelton (c. 1460–1529) for the court of Henry VIII. Secular
counsel is the main concern of the play. The hero, Magnyfycence,
who in his potential for good and evil represents the young Henry
VIII, is a combination of the Aristotelian virtues μεγαλοπρεπέια
and μεγαλοψυχία, Magnificence and Greatness of Soul. The other
court figures are Felycyte, Lyberte and Measure, each misused at
the expense of Magnyfycence by Counterfet Countenance, Crafty
Conveyance, Clokyd Colusyon and Courtly Abusyon, and finally
restored by Redresse, Circumspeccyon and Perseverance. The four
Vices are caricatures of those aspects of Renaissance power politics
which in Elizabethan times came to be particularly associated with
the name of Machiavelli, and I find no difficulty in accepting that
all four represent aspects of Wolsey's policy and behaviour as seen
through the somewhat jaundiced eyes of Skelton. The clustered
C's of their names may refer to the cardinalate obtained by Wolsey
in 1515. All four disguise themselves to become counsellors –
Crafty Conveyance as Sure Surveyance, Counterfet Countenance
as Good Demeanance, Clokyd Colusyon as Sober Sadness,
Courtly Abusyon as Lusty Pleasure – and it is because he follows
their advice that Magnyfycence is reduced to poverty and despair.

Sir David Lindsay (c. 1488–1555) combined the morality form
with the cause of the early Reformers and the internal problems of
Scottish political and social life in *Ane Pleasant Satyre of the Thrie
Estaitis in Commendatioun of Vertew and Vituperatioun of Vyce*, to
give the title in its full form, which equally emphasizes satire and
moral allegory. The play was perhaps written in or about 1535,
but it was not certainly performed until 1552. It is not so much a
satire on King James V as a call for him to reform the country at all
levels, and especially to sweep away Church abuses. Much less

dramatically effective, but even more a part of the Reformation, is *John, King of England* (c. 1540), by the protestant Bishop of Ossory, John Bale (1495–1563), a play which gives a more or less historical account of the reign of King John, but at the same time interprets the historical figures under such satirical morality names as Private Wealth and Usurped Power, and points firmly to the parallel between events in John's reign and those of the Reformation.

The morality play, as those last examples show, had a power not shared by the miracle cycles to survive the Reformation. Moralities in fact, were the staple dramatic fare of Marlowe, Shakespeare and Jonson in their youth. In addition, much of their general reading must have fostered a natural tendency towards allegory of many different kinds. The morality structure, with its frequent satiric and realistic overtones, and the general allegorical ambience of so many among their plays – *The Jew of Malta, Doctor Faustus, As You Like It, Henry IV, Measure for Measure, Volpone,* to name no others – is perhaps the greatest single contribution of allegory to the literature of England.

Bibliography

For editions generally, the reader is referred to the standard bibliographies and works of reference. Most of the books listed below contain a bibliography.

E. AUERBACH, *Mimesis. The Representation of Reality in Western Literature*, tr. W. R. Trask, Princeton, 1953.

Scenes from the Drama of European Literature, New York, 1959.

J. A. W. BENNETT, *The Parlement of Foules. An Interpretation*, Oxford, 1957.

Chaucer's Book of Fame. An Exposition of 'The House of Fame.' Oxford, 1968.

M. W. BLOOMFIELD, *The Seven Deadly Sins. An Introduction to the History of a Religious Concept with Special Reference to Medieval English Literature*, East Lansing, 1952.

Piers Plowman as a Fourteenth-century Apocalypse, New Brunswick, 1961.

R. BOSSUAT, *Alain de Lille. Anticlaudianus*, Paris, 1955.

E. DE BRUYNE, *Etudes d' Esthétique Médiévale*, 3 vols., Bruges, 1946. See especially Vol. III.

G. B. CAIRD, *The Revelation of St. John the Divine*, London, 1966.

E. R. CURTIUS, *European Literature and the Latin Middle Ages*, tr. W. R. Trask, London, 1953.

C.H. DODD, *The Parables of the Kingdom*, 2nd edit., London, 1961.

E. R. DODDS, *The Greeks and the Irrational*, Berkeley and Los Angeles, 1951.

D. L. DREW, *The Allegory of the Aeneid*, London, 1927.

A. FLETCHER, *Allegory. The Theory of a Symbolic Mode*, Ithaca, 1964.

A. FOWLER, *Spenser and the Numbers of Time,* London, 1964.

N. FRYE, 'Ethical Criticism: Theory of Symbols', the second essay in *Anatomy of Criticism,* Princeton, 1957.

J. A. GILES, *Opuscula Scientifica,* Vol. VI of *Venerabilis Bedae Opera,* London, 1843. (Contains *De Schematibus et Tropis Sacrae Scripturae, De Temporibus* and *De Temporum Ratione.*)

W. K. C. GUTHRIE, *Orpheus and Greek Religion,* London, 1935.

K. HIEATT, *Short Time's Endless Monument. The Symbolism of the Numbers in Edmund Spenser's 'Epithalamion',* New York, 1960.

E. HONIG, *Dark Conceit. The Making of Allegory,* London, 1959.

G. HOUGH, *A Preface to the Faerie Queene,* London, 1962. See especially Chapter VI, 'Allegory in The Faerie Queene'.

W. W. JACKSON, *Dante's Convivio Translated into English,* Oxford, 1909.

G. R. DE LAGE, *Alain de Lille. Poète du XIIe Siècle,* Montreal and Paris, 1951.

J. LAWLOR, *Piers Plowman. An Essay in Criticism,* London, 1962. See especially Chapter VI, 'Allegory, Similitude and Wordplay'.

C. S. LEWIS, *The Allegory of Love,* Oxford, 1936.

R. S. LOOMIS, ed., *Arthurian Literature in the Middle Ages,* Oxford, 1959.

H. DE LUBAC, *Exégèse Médiévale,* 4 vols., Paris, 1959–63.

J. MACQUEEN, 'Tradition and the Interpretation of the *Kingis Quair*', *R.E.S.* xii (1961), pp. 117–31.
'*As You Like It* and Mediaeval Literary Tradition', *Forum,* i(1965), pp. 216–29.
'Ane Satyre of the Thrie Estaitis', *Studies in Scottish Literature,* iii(1966), pp. 129–43.
Robert Henryson. A Study of the Major Narrative Poems, Oxford, 1967.

É. MÂLE, *The Gothic Image. Religious Art in France of the Thirteenth Century*, Tr. D. Nussey, London, 1961. (First published in English as *Religious Art in France: XIII Century. A Study in Mediaeval Iconography and its Sources of Inspiration*, London, 1913.)

C. MOORMAN, "'The Tale of the Sankgreall". Human Frailty', Chapter VI of *Malory's Originality. A Critical Study of Le Morte Darthur*, ed. R. M. Lumiansky, Baltimore, 1964.

G. MURRAY, *Five Stages of Greek Religion*, London, 1935. See especially the Appendix.

C. MUSCATINE, 'The Emergence of Psychological Allegory in Old French Romance', *P.M.L.A.*, lxviii (1953), pp. 1160–82.

C. G. OSGOOD, *Boccaccio on Poetry*, Princeton, 1930.

G. R. OWST, *Literature and Pulpit in Medieval England*, 2nd edit., Oxford, 1961.

A. A. PARKER, *Literature and the Delinquent. The Picaresque Novel in Spain and Europe, 1599–1753*, Edinburgh, 1967.

D. W. ROBINSON, Jr., *A Preface to Chaucer. Studies in Medieval Perspectives*, Oxford, 1963. Valuable material, but the book as a whole is to be used with extreme caution and scepticism.

E. SALTER, *Piers Plowman. An Introduction*, Oxford, 1962. See especially Chapter III, 'The Allegory of *Piers Plowman*; Nature and Meaning.'

J. SEZNEC, *The Survival of the Pagan Gods. The Mythological Tradition and its Place in Renaissance Humanism and Art*, New York, 1953.

B. SMALLEY, *The Study of the Bible in the Middle Ages*, 2nd edit., Oxford 1952.

C. SPICQ, *Esquisse d'une Histoire de l'Exégèse Latine au Moyen Age*, Paris, 1944.

W. H. STAHL, *Macrobius. Commentary on the Dream of Scipio Translated with an Introduction and Notes*, New York and London, 1952.

P. TOYNBEE, *Dantis Alagherii Epistolae, The Letters of Dante,* Oxford, 1920. The letter to Can Grande della Scala is Epistle X.

R. TUVE, *Allegorical Imagery. Some Mediaeval Books and their Posterity,* Princeton, 1966.

E. VINAVER, *The Works of Sir Thomas Malory,* single volume edition, London, 1954. References are to this edition.

Acknowledgements

I am indebted to the General Editor of this series, Professor J. D. Jump, for much assistance and kindness.

Miss E. M. Brown, Miss Nan V. Dunbar, and my colleagues Mrs Anna Belfourd, Mr. I. M. Campbell, Mr. J. B. Ellis, and Dr. R. D. S. Jack have allowed me to benefit from their knowledge and experience. I am grateful to my wife who has helped me in many ways, not least by preparing the index.

Index

ning